EDITOR: LEE JOHNSON

 OSPREY MILITARY

NEW VANGUARD

IS-2
HEAVY TANK
1944-1973

Text by
STEVE ZALOGA
Colour plates by
PETER SARSON

First published in Great Britain in 1994 by
Osprey, an imprint of Reed Consumer Books Ltd.
Michelin House, 81 Fulham Road,
London SW3 6RB
and Auckland, Melbourne, Singapore and Toronto

ISBN 1 85532 396 6

Filmset in Great Britain
Printed through Bookbuilders Ltd, Hong Kong

Acknowledgements
The author would like to thank a number of friends and colleagues for their help in preparing this book. First and
foremost to Janusz Magnuski for his extensive aid in tracing
Soviet heavy tank history. Thanks to the staff of the Kubinka
armour museum for access to their superb collection, examples of which are shown for the first time in photographs
here. Thanks also to Bob Fleming at the Budge Collection
for access to the many interesting examples of Soviet heavy
armour in their collection. Thanks to Stephen Sewell for help
with the many new Russian publications on the Stalin tanks.
Acknowledgements also go to Joseph Bermudez and Sam
Katz for help in tracing the foreign use of Stalin heavy tanks.
Special thanks also go to many colleagues in Russia and
Belorussia for help in supplying photographs and drawings.

Editor's note
Readers may wish to study this title in conjunction with the
following Osprey titles:

New Vanguard 1 *Kingtiger*
New Vanguard 5 *Tiger I*
Campaign 16 *Kursk 1943*
MAA 216 *The Red Army of the Great Patriotic War*
MAA 117 *The Polish Army 1939-45*
MAA 127 *The Israeli Army in the Middle East Wars*
MAA 128 *Arab Armies of the Middle East Wars 1948-73*

Author's note
The Stalin series is properly designated 'IS' in English, based
on the proper transliteration of Iosef Stalin. They have been
known for many years as the JS Stalin heavy tanks, in part
due to the English spelling of Joseph, but also due to Anglo-
American reliance on wartime German intelligence reports
about these tanks which used the proper German transliteration of Stalin's name, Josef.

DEVELOPMENTAL HISTORY

The Iosef Stalin tanks were the ultimate heavy tanks developed by the Soviet Union. The IS-2 Stalin tank was popularly called the 'Victory tank' in Russia due to its close association with the defeat of Germany in 1945. The sleek and elegant lines of the IS-3 Stalin tank of 1945 heavily influenced post-war tank design, not only in the Soviet Union, but in Europe and America as well. During the Cold War years of the 1950s, no tank was so dreaded by NATO as the T-10 tank, the final evolution of the Stalin series. Yet in spite of their reputation in the West, the Stalin tanks emerged from a troubled design, had a brief moment of glory in 1944 and 1945, and disappeared in ignominy after 1960. It has only been possible in recent years to tell their true story.

The KV series

The Iosef Stalin IS heavy tanks evolved from the earlier KV series. By the autumn of 1942, the KV-1 heavy tanks were widely regarded in the Red Army and the Soviet government as a failed design. During assessments of the disastrous combat failures in the Kharkov battles and the Crimean campaign in the summer of 1942, the KV tank was roundly criticised for its technical and tactical shortcomings. At 47 tons, the KV was substantially heavier than the 28-ton T-34 medium tank. In combat the tank brigades often temporarily lost their KV tanks when they encountered bridges that could not withstand their weight. In addition the KV-1's slow speed and unreliable performance compared badly with the excellent combat characteristics of the T-34 medium tank. In contrast to German heavy tanks, which were invariably more heavily armed than their medium tanks, the KV-1 was equipped with

The KV-13 was an attempt by SKB-2 to develop a 'universal tank' that would replace both the T-34 medium tank and the KV heavy tank. It was shorter in length than the normal KV-1. The KV-13 was a failure, but the hull configuration was used on the IS-1 Stalin heavy tank.

the same 76mm gun as the T-34. The KV-1's sole advantage was its heavier armour, which did not compensate for its shortcomings.

At a meeting of the State Defence Committee (GKO) in the autumn of 1942, several military leaders urged that KV production be halted and that their production facilities be shifted to the T-34 tank. Representatives of the tank industry argued that this would disrupt production. As a compromise, it was agreed to shift all KV tanks out of the normal tank brigades, and concentrate them in independent heavy tank regiments. Production of the 'Tankograd' plant in Chelyabinsk which manufactured the KV was partially shifted to T-34 production. In addition, the tank industry was instructed by Stalin that the technical shortcomings of the KV be solved or that the parties involved would suffer the consequences.

Development of the KV heavy tanks was undertaken by SKB-2 (Special Design Bureau-2), headed by Gen. Zh. Kotin at the massive Tankograd plant in Chelyabinsk[1]. During the summer of 1942, Kotin's team had concentrated its attention

[1]This plant was officially called the Kirov Plant No. 100, but became known as Tankograd (Tank City) due to its huge size.

The final production variant of the KV series was the KV-85. This was a stop-gap improvisation, mating the new turret from the IS-85 tank with a modified KV-1S chassis. The new IS-85 turret had a wider turret ring than the KV-1S, so a fillet had to be added to the hull sides to provide the added space.

on the KV-13 'universal tank'. The KV-13 was an attempt to reduce the weight of the KV down to the 30 ton range while retaining armour thick enough to stop the German 88mm gun. It was Kotin's hope that the KV-13 would prove so successful that it would replace both the T-34 and the KV tank in production, hence the term 'universal tank'. Considerable pressure was placed on Kotin, since orders had already been received from Moscow to begin shifting a portion of Tankograd's production to the rival T-34 medium tank. There was a real fear that KV production would be totally halted, and the design bureau

closed. During trials in the late summer of 1942, it became evident that the KV-13 suffered from the traditional 'Achilles heel' of the KV family, an unreliable transmission. As a result, the project was cancelled. Kotin was devastated by the failure, and colleagues recall that for days he sat and stared blankly into space.

The KV programme was retrieved by a second modernisation programme headed by the assistant head of the bureau, Nikolai Dukhov. The poor transmission was the most significant technical weakness of the KV design. Dukhov mated an improved transmission designed in 1941 for the ill-fated KV-3 design by Nikolai Shashmurin, along with a lightened hull and modified turret. This vehicle, the KV-1S (S–*skorotsknoi*, fast), reduced the armoured protection of the KV-1 in favour of increased reliability and speed. It was accepted for production in August 1942 to replace the failed KV-1.

The KV-1S proved to be a short-lived stop-gap. In January 1943, the Red Army captured an example of the new Tiger I heavy tank in the Leningrad area. The Tiger I had superior armour

The IS-85 entered production at the end of 1943. It was a very short-lived type as it was decided to re-arm the tank with a 122mm gun. This shows the classic IS-85 features: the KV-13 hull front, the narrow mantlet and the 85mm gun. This tank was later redesignated IS-1.

to the KV-1S and, with the potent 88mm gun, superior firepower as well. In the summer of 1943, the Germans also introduced the new Panther medium tank with an excellent new long-barrelled 75mm gun that was vastly superior to the short 76mm gun being used on the Soviet T-34 and KV tanks. Ironically, the great tank battles at Kursk were won by the Red Army at a time when their tank force was qualitatively weakest against the Germans. At no previous time during the war had the Germans enjoyed such clear technological advantage over the Soviet tank force. German Tiger units were able to decimate Soviet tank units before the T-34s and KV-1S tanks were even in range. Fortunately for the Red Army, Tiger and Panther tanks were still few in numbers and the Panther, in particular, suffered from the technical teething pains common in many new tanks.

Izdeliye 237

The capture of the German Tiger tank in January 1943 led to the decision to begin work on a new heavy tank, codenamed *izdeliye* 237 (Item-237). The KV tank had been named after Kotin's father-in-law, the pre-war defence minister Klimenti Voroshilov. Voroshilov had fallen from favour in 1941 as a result of his bungling leadership of the Red Army. So Kotin felt it prudent to rename the new tank, and chose the obvious solution, Iosef Stalin, in order to curry favour with the Soviet dictator. The new tank design team, codenamed 'Bureau IS', was managed by Nikolai Shashmurin, whose transmission design had saved the KV-1S. Also on the team were several other experienced designers including A. Yermolayev, L. Sychev and N. Rybin. The development effort started by conducting ballistic trials against the captured German Tiger tank. The Tiger was subjected to fire from 76mm tank guns using new ammunition, from 122mm howitzers, 85mm anti-aircraft guns and 122mm corps guns. Both the 85mm anti-aircraft gun and 122mm corps gun gave good performance against the Tiger, and there were hopes that new anti-tank projectiles could further improve their performance. The effort to adapt the 85mm anti-aircraft gun to tanks was handed over to Gen. F. Petrov's design bureau in Sverdlovsk.

The izdeliye 240 was the prototype for the IS-2 series. It used an A-19 122mm gun with a single baffle muzzle brake. The production IS-122 used a double baffle brake.

The izd.237 design took advantage of earlier work on the KV-13 and KV-1S. The forward hull design was essentially the same as the KV-13, but the engine compartment was modernised and a more reliable transmission was added. The new hull design dispensed with the fifth crewman, leaving only the driver in the forward part of the hull. The turret used the improved layout of the KV-1S, with the commander and gunner in the left side of the turret, and the loader in the right. The new turret had heavier armour than the KV-1S, as well as improved optics. While Shashmurin's team had been working on the izd.237 prototype since June, another team at Chelyabinsk under N. Dukhov was exploring the possibility of uparming the KV-1S with the new 85mm gun, and at least one prototype was constructed, but the turret was too small to accommodate the gun properly.

KV-85

The intense tank fighting in the summer of 1943 led to bitter complaints from Soviet tank commanders about the poor firepower of the T-34 and KV tanks. The new izd.237 heavy tank was not expected to be ready until the end of the year. None the less, there was pressure to do something to redress the firepower balance. Dukhov's team was instructed to mount the improved turret for the izd.237 on to the KV-1S hull, called the KV-85. This required the hull to be widened due to

An early production IS-122 in combat in the summer of 1944. The original production batch of the IS-122 used the KV-13 hull front, the narrow gun mantlet and the early 'gum-drop' gunner's periscope on the roof.

the greater diameter of the new turret. The easiest way to do this was to add a pair of fillets on either side. This was hardly ideal, but the tank was regarded as a stop-gap. In August 1943, the proto-types of the izd.237 and the KV-85 were demonstrated at the Kubinka proving ground to Stalin and the members of the GKO. Stalin authorized the immediate production of the KV-85, and instructed that the izd.237 be rushed into production as soon as possible as the IS-85 heavy tank. The KV-85 entered production at Chelyabinsk in September and by November about 130 were completed.

IS-85

Production efforts on the IS-85 at Chelyabinsk started in September, but required far more extensive effort than the KV-85. For example, the new hull required a large casting; the improved suspension experienced some problems as well. The production programme was also delayed over the issue of its armament. By the autumn of 1943, the Red Army was becoming convinced that the

76mm gun on the T-34 was inadequate, and so had already begun a programme to up-gun this vehicle as well. This was disheartening news to the Chelyabinsk designers, as it implied that once again, their tank would be no better armed than the standard Red Army medium tank. Firing trials of the new D-5T 85mm gun also had also proved disappointing. Several captured German Tiger I tanks were shipped to Chelyabinsk, where they

The second production batch of IS-122 retained the KV-13 hull front, but introduced a new turret fitted with an improved and wider main gun mantlet. This particular vehicle is preserved at the Polish Armed Forces Museum in Warsaw.

An example of the interim IS-122 variant in combat with the 2nd Ukrainian Front in the outskirts of Budapest, Hungary, in December 1944. This vehicle has the early hull front, but the improved, widened mantlet.

were subjected to 85mm fire from various angles. The 85mm gun could not reliably penetrate the Tiger I except at ranges within the lethal envelope of the Tiger I's own 88mm gun. The solution was to mount a heavier gun in the izd.237. Petrov's bureau favoured the new D-10 100mm gun being developed by his bureau specifically for tank fighting. However, it was unlikely to be ready in time and ammunition supply would also be a problem since it represented a new gun calibre for the Red Army. Ammunition for the 122mm corps gun was already in the Red Army's supply network, so this calibre was selected for a new design, the izd.240. This project was approved in November 1943, just as the first izd.237s were coming off the production lines. The izd.237s were accepted for service as the IS-85. A total of 67 IS-85s were completed by the end of 1943, and 40 more at the beginning of 1944.

The Petrov artillery design team completed a crash programme to adapt the A-19 122mm corps gun to the same mounting used by the D-5T 85mm tank gun. The new 122mm tank gun was called the D-25T. The first samples shipped to Chelyabinsk in late November 1943 used a traditional artillery screw-breech. A more efficient semi-automatic drop-breech was also in development for the series production vehicles. The

prototype guns were mounted into the izd.240 prototype and shipped to the Kubinka proving ground for trials at the end of November. The target was a captured German Panther tank. From a range of 1500 metres, the 122mm round penetrated the glacis plate, passed through the tank's engine, and pierced the rear plate as well. As a result of the success of these trials the decision was made to produce the izd.240 as soon as possible. The modifications on the D-25T gun were completed in December, leading to official acceptance of the design on 31 December 1943.

The IS-1 and IS-2

Production of the izd.240 was begun in January 1944, and the new design was called the IS-122. It was soon decided to simplify the designations for security purposes, with the izd.237 becoming the IS-1 and the izd.240 becoming the IS-2. Production of the first IS-2 Stalin heavy tanks was slow due to the lack of guns and the complexity of the design. The first 150 were finished in February, followed by 275 in March. Production of the T-34 was halted at Chelyabinsk in April in order to increase IS-2 production, which reached 350 that month. A new assembly hall was added at the Tankograd complex, and this began to have effect during the second quarter of the year.

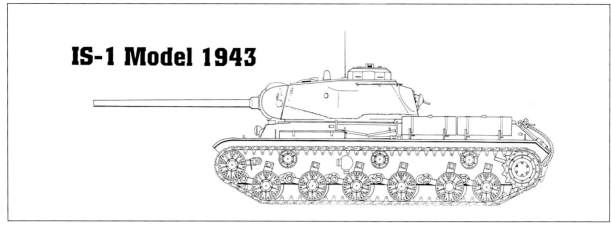

IS-1 Model 1943

IS-2 Model 1944

0   1   2   3
METER

© Steven J. Zaloga 1993

The definitive IS-2 appeared in the spring of 1944, introducing a new forward hull casting. This version is sometimes called the IS-2m or IS-2 Model

1944. This tank passes through Poznan, Poland in January 1945. Notice that the fourth road wheel is missing, probably from mine damage.

OPERATIONAL HISTORY

It is not clear if any IS-1 tanks were actually issued to combat units. In the event, it was decided to rebuild most of them as IS-2s, and at least 102 were reconfigured with the 122mm gun. As the new IS-2 tanks became available in February 1944, special new tank units were formed for them. These units were designated as separate Guards heavy tank regiments (OGTTP: *otdelniy gvardeiskiy tyazheliy tankoviy polk*), and had a total of 21 IS-2 tanks formed into four companies with five tanks each. These regiments were sometimes called 'breakthrough regiments' by the Germans as they were usually reserved for special offensive operations. They were often used to

The only other army to use the IS-2 in combat in the Second World War was the Polish LWP. Here, a tank of the 4th Heavy Tank Regiment crosses a damaged bridge that has been repaired by filling it with fascines.

spearhead tank attacks through heavily protected German defensive positions at the outset of major offensive operations. Until they became available in larger numbers, the IS-2s were concentrated in special High Command reserve units.

Into battle

The first known operational use of the IS-2 took place in April 1944 when the newly formed 11th Seperate Guards Heavy Tank Regiment commanded by Col. Tsiganov fought several skirmishes with the Tiger I tanks of the s.Pz.Abt. 503 near Tarnopol. A single IS-2 was knocked out, but the Germans had little time to examine their new adversary before being forced to retreat. The Wehrmacht got a closer look a month later near the Rumanian town of Tirgu Frumos. At least one IS-2 regiment was used during a Soviet offensive operation in·May 1944 in Romania, a strategic feint intended to distract the Germans from the main offensive in Belorussia. The IS-2 heavy tanks came as a surprise to the German troops in

the area who had never encountered a Soviet tank capable of engaging them with such heavy firepower at ranges of over 3,000 metres. A company of Tiger I tanks from Panzer Grenadier Division Grossdeutschland opened fire at 3,000 metres, and were shocked to see their 88mm rounds harmlessly ricochet off the thick frontal armour of the IS-2s. A counter-attack by Hptm. B. Klemz's company knocked out three IS-2 heavy tanks, and resulted in Klemz's decoration with the Knight's Cross. The Germans concluded that the new Stalin heavy tank regiment was very inexperienced.

An IS-2 in the streets of Berlin during the final fighting. The white turret band and white roof cross were allied identification markings introduced to avoid Allied aircraft from strafing Red Army tank formations.

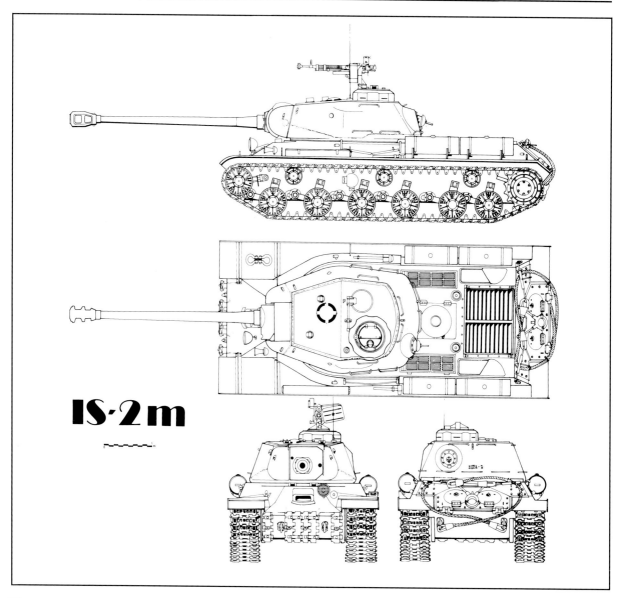

IS·2m

The Tiger crews were able to inspect the disabled Stalins and concluded that they were well armed, well armoured, but somewhat slow and unmanoeuvrable compared to the Tiger I. After this small skirmish in Romania, Stalin tanks began showing up in increasing numbers all along the Eastern Front.

The inexperienced new heavy tank regiments had little immediate impact on the fighting, but the new tanks were a welcome addition to Soviet tank formations. Indeed, the applause from tankers led to the decision to expand production as rapidly as possible to permit each tank corps to receive at least one regiment of IS-2s. During Operation Bagration in Belorussia, the most critical operation of the early summer, the separate Guards heavy tank regiments were still very few in number. Even for this crucial offensive, only four IS-2 regiments could be allotted: 2 OGTTP (1st Baltic Front); 14 and 35 OGTTP (3rd Belorussian Front) and 30 OGTPP (1st Belorussian Front). Two of these regiments were honoured for their superior performance in the summer fighting by being named in honour of cities they helped liberate, becoming the 2nd Polotskiy OGTTP and the 30th Brestskiy OGTTP. Opera-

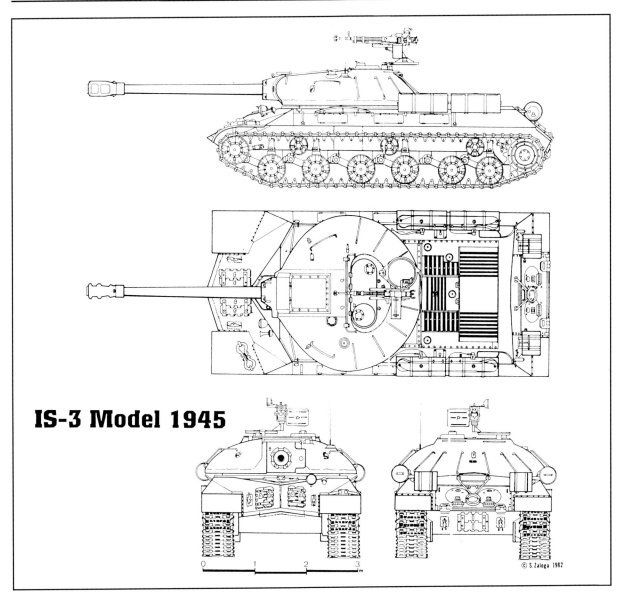

IS-3 Model 1945

0 1 2 3
m

© S. Zaloga 1982

tion Bagration led to the destruction of the German Army Group Centre, the single most decisive rout of a German army group during the course of the war. This critical victory brought the Red Army to the outskirts of Warsaw.

Soviet heavy tank tactics

In some respects, the IS-2 Stalin heavy tanks were used like the German Tiger I heavy tanks. That is, they were organized in small, independent units allotted to the high command for special missions. The German Tiger battalions were typically used as defensive 'fire brigades', rapidly moved along the front to stem particularly serious Soviet breakthroughs. In contrast, the IS-2s were mainly used to support breakthroughs. As often as not, Soviet commanders picked a breakthrough location where German tank strength was especially weak. As a result, IS-2 Stalin tanks did not necessarily see a great deal of tank-vs.-tank fighting. Their armour and firepower were potent tools in intimidating the weakly supported German infantry. Their main adversaries were German infantry anti-tank teams, armed with panzerfaust and panzerschreck anti-tank rockets and the towed 75mm PaK 40 anti-tank gun.

11

A fine overview of a Polish IS-2 Model 1944 giving a clear view of its layout. The five 'X's on the barrel are kill markings signifying its wartime record.

Beginning in 1954, the IS-2s were modernised as the IS-2M. This modernization included the addition of stowage boxes on the hull side, new side skirts, additional external fuel stowage and many internal improvements. This superbly restored example was handed over to the Imperial War Museum collection at Duxford Airfield in 1988, where it is currently displayed.

The demand for greater production of IS-2 tanks led to a number of changes in the design. The front hull design, based on the KV-13, proved awkward to manufacture. A new cast bow was developed in the spring of 1944 to remedy this. In addition, the mantlet and trunnion mounting for the D-25T gun, first developed for the smaller and less powerful D-5T 85mm gun, was not durable enough. A new wider mantlet was introduced. Other small changes were also made including the substitution of the MK 4 periscope for the older PT-4-17, and the addition of a 12.7mm DShK heavy machine gun for vehicle

defence. This improved version was called IS-2m or IS-2 Model 1944. Production of the IS-2 at the Tankograd plant amounted to 2,250: 250 in the first quarter of 1944, 525 in the second, 725 in the third and 750 in the last.

The Stalin's adversaries – The Panther

Performance comparisons between the IS-2 and German Second World War tanks show some significant differences in design philosophy. Although termed a heavy tank by the Russians, the IS-2 in fact was more similar in size and weight to the German Panther medium tank, each having a combat weight of about 46 tons. In overall terms, the IS-2 and Panther were a fairly close match in anti-tank firepower. But the Panther carried significantly more rounds of ammunition, 81 rounds against 28 in the Stalin. This difference was a consequence of the Soviet selection of the 122mm gun, which had larger and heavier ammunition rounds than the German long 75mm gun. Both the German and Soviet tank guns had similar anti-armour penetration at 1,000 metres (150-160mm), the German projectile being very small and light at 4.7 kg while the Soviet round was a huge 25 kg.[1] The Soviet gun had a distinct advantage when used in fire support against non-armoured targets, being able to deliver a 25 kg high-explosive projectile compared to the Panther's puny 7 kg. Although tank enthusiasts are obsessed with the anti-armour performance of tank guns, based on historical record far more rounds of high-explosive are used by tanks in combat. The IS-2 Stalin had significant advantage over the Panther in terms of armour both on the turret front (160mm against 110mm) and hull front (120mm against 90mm). The Soviet advantage came at the expense of internal volume, another reason why the IS-2 carried so few rounds of ammunition. According to German tactical instructions, a Panther had to close to 600 metres to guarantee penetration of IS-2 while the IS-2 could penetrate the Panther at ranges of 1,000 metres. They could penetrate each others side

[1] It should be remembered that kinetic energy on impact is more dependent on speed than mass (kinetic energy= mass x velocity2/ballistic and gravitational effect). The German round, with a muzzle velocity of 1120m/s, had similar energy on impact to the larger Soviet round which had a muzzle velocity of only 781 m/s.

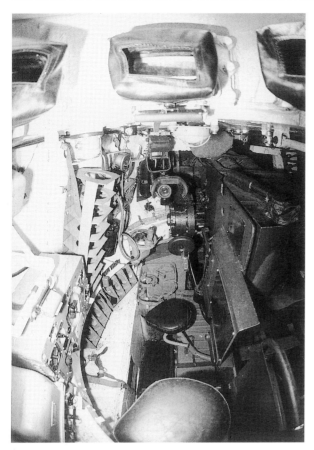

as much ammunition as the IS-2. Both tanks could knock each other out at normal combat ranges of 1,000 metres. At longer ranges, the capabilities of both tanks were dependent on the crews and battlefield conditions. The thicker frontal armour of the IS-2 protected it against Tiger I fire at ranges over 1500 metres while the Tiger I was still vulnerable to IS-2 fire. However, the German tank enjoyed markedly better optical equipment than the Soviet tank, a feature which influenced any long-range engagements. The relative advantages and disadvantages of both tanks meant that victory in tank combat was most often dictated by the tactical situation and crew performance.

The interior of the IS-2 is relatively spacious by Soviet standards. This is a view from the commander's station looking down towards the gunner's station in front of him. The breech of the D-25T 122mm gun is to the right. The stowage racks in front of the radio are for 7.62mm ammunition drums.

armour at ranges of 2,000 metres. The Panther was a more nimble tank, with a power-to-weight ratio of 15.4 hp/ton to the Stalin's 11.3 hp/ton and a top speed of 46 km/h against 37 km/h.

Tiger I

In comparison to the Tiger I, the IS-2 had modest advantages in armour, even though it was ten tons lighter. The main reason for this was again that the IS-2 was very cramped compared to the Tiger I. In terms of firepower, the 88mm gun on the Tiger I was similar in overall anti-armour firepower to the IS-2's 122mm gun, and the IS-2 had advantages when firing high-explosive ammunition against unarmoured targets due to its larger projectile. The Tiger I carried more than three times

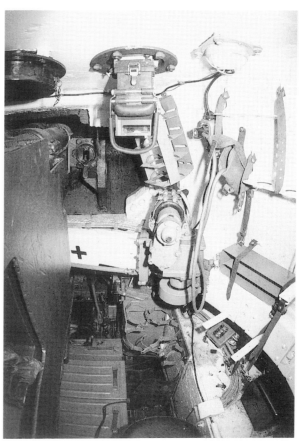

The loader sits in the right side of the IS-2 turret. The breech of the 122mm gun is to the left and on the floor is stowage for projectiles and their separate propellant cases. On this vehicle, the co-axial 7.62mm machine gun is not fitted.

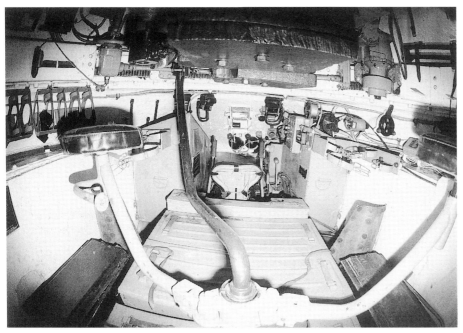

A floor-level view from the rear of the IS-2 fighting compartment towards the driver's compartment. The centre conduit carries electrical cables to the turret while the two side supports are for the seats of the gunner and loader. The boxes on the hull floor are primarily used for stowage of the ammunition propellant. The 122mm D-25T uses two piece ammunition due to its heavy weight: a 13 lb propellant case and a 55 lb armour-piercing projectile.

Tiger II

In August 1944, a new adversary appeared on the Eastern Front, the Königstiger heavy tank, also called the Tiger II or King Tiger. At 68 tons, the Tiger II was considerably larger and heavier than the IS-2 Stalin. The first combat encounter between Soviet tanks and the Tiger II took place on 12 August 1944 when a T-34/85 of the 53rd Guards Tank Brigade ambushed a column from s.Pz.Abt. 501 near the small Polish village of Ogledow and knocked out three Tiger IIs.

Encounters between the Tiger II and the IS-2 appear to have been rare, if for no other reason than the small number of Tiger IIs that actually saw service in the East. There were occasional encounters between s.Pz.Abt. 503 and IS-2 regiments in Hungary in November 1944 outside Budapest. One of the largest encounters took place on 12 January 1945 during the opening phases of the Soviet Oder offensive. A column of Tiger IIs from s.Pz.Abt. 524 were involved in a short-range engagement with Stalin tanks near the village of Lisow, with both the German and Soviet formations suffering heavy losses in a savage firefight.

A comparison between the IS-2 and the Tiger II is not particularly fair due to the enormous size and weight difference in the German tank's favour. The Tiger II was better armoured than the IS-2, and its gun was significantly superior in anti-armour penetration, especially at longer ranges. The IS-2's only advantage was its slightly better mobility. It is noteworthy that the most successful engagements between the IS-2 and Tiger II were at very close ranges where the Tiger II's firepower and armour advantages were less relevant.

China was one of the largest users of IS-2 heavy tanks after the Second World War. Indeed, the presence of IS-2 heavy tanks on the China-Indochina border in 1952-3 considerably worried French forces fighting the Viet-Minh guerrilla movement.

A view of the rear of the fighting compartment. The stowage racks immediately behind the loader are for the long BR-471 armour-piercing or OF-462 high explosive rounds. The racks behind the commander have a spacer at the bottom to accommodate the shorter APC-T or HEAT projectiles. This is an IS-2M interior, evident from the black, circular ventilator fan at the rear of the compartment behind the commander, which replaced a 7.62mm DTM machine gun on the earlier IS-2 Model 1944.

The shortcomings of the IS-2 in combat with German tanks led to several improvement efforts. The small ammunition load on the IS-2 was a significant tactical hindrance in combat, especially when involved in breakthrough operations where large numbers of German anti-tank guns and strongpoints were encountered. The obvious solution was to mount a long-barrelled 85mm gun or 100mm gun which offered the anti-tank performance of the D-25T, but which would permit a larger ammunition load. The original IS-1 carried double the ammunition load of the IS-2, 59 rounds against 28, due to the smaller volume of the 85mm ammunition. The 85mm gun was reconsidered on the izd.244 prototype, using the improved S-53 gun. However, the anti-armour performance of this weapon was not adequate. The izd.245 and izd.248 were fitted with new 100mm guns. Although the ballistic performance of the new D-10 100mm gun was superior to the 122mm D-25T in the anti-armour role, the problem still remained that there was a surplus of 122mm gun tubes and 122mm ammunition production capacity, and an inadequate supply for the 100mm gun alternative. This approach was therefore rejected in spite of its technical merits.

In December 1944, the availability of large number of IS-2s from Tankograd allowed the formation of the first Guards heavy tank brigades. These were equipped with 65 IS-2 tanks, 3 SU-76 light assault guns, 19 armoured transporters and 3 BA-64 armoured cars. These brigades were few in number, and reserved for use by armies and fronts during breakthrough operations. They were specifically intended for assaults on fortified lines with heavy infantry and engineer support. The

The IS-3 Stalin tank was first seen in public in a September 1945 victory parade in Berlin. Although it has long been claimed that the IS-3 saw combat in the Berlin campaign, recently declassified Russian accounts dispute this.

The IS-3M was a modernised IS-3, most clearly distinguishable by the new side skirts along the hull. This ex-Egyptian IS-3M was captured by the Israeli Army in the Sinai during the 1967 war. The IS-3M was the only tank genuinely feared by Israeli troops, as its thick frontal armour made it very difficult to defeat in combat.

first of these brigades was ready in time for the January 1945 Oder offensive when the Red Army thrust into the heart of Germany. Expanded IS-2 production also permitted each tank corps to be allotted an IS-2 heavy tank regiment, each with 21 heavy tanks.

New designs – IS-3

With IS-2 production well under way, two separate new heavy tank efforts began. Gen. Nikolai Dukhov led a team on a project codenamed Kirovets-1 which was intended to develop a heavy tank resistant to the fire from the long 88mm gun on the Tiger II. One of his engineers had conducted a study on tank vulnerability that concluded that the hits on the turret front were most often the cause of tank loss, followed by hits on the hull front. As a result, a radical new shape was designed. The turret was a simple hemisphere with a thick armour gun mantlet faired cleanly into the shape. The hull panels were cleverly laid

In contrast to the IS-2, the IS-3 interior is very cramped due to the steeply sloping sides of the cast turret. This is a view of the gunner's station in an

IS-3M showing the manual controls. The gunner's telescopic and periscopic sights are missing in this view.

The IS-4 heavy tank was produced in small numbers in the late 1940s, and most were shipped to the Far East in anticipation of intervention in the Korean War. This vehicle, currently preserved at the Kubinka armour museum near Moscow, shows its physical similarity to the IS-2. It was the heaviest tank series ever produced in the USSR.

out to increase their effective thickness to frontal attack by heavily angling them. To accommodate the large turret, the upper hull sides actually sloped inward, a feature hidden by attaching thin metal tool stowage bins along the upper sides. Internally, the Kirovets-1 was essentially similar to the IS-2, using a slightly modified V-11-IS-3 engine without the inertia starter of the older engine. It also used the same main gun. Unlike the IS-2 which had a large turret bustle to stow ammunition, the Kirovets-1 stowed projectiles along the thick walls of the turret interior.

The prototype of the Kirovets-1 was completed in October 1944, and it was accepted for series production as the IS-3. Production of the IS-3 began at Chelyabinsk in 1945 in parallel to the IS-2m. The IS-3 design had been prematurely rushed into production, and the tank was beset with scores of mechanical problems. As a result, no significant number of IS-3s were ready before the end of the war in Europe. The issue of whether or not the IS-3 saw any fighting in the

The IS-6 was an abortive attempt to develop an electrical transmission for heavy tanks. The project was a failure, and a mechanical transmission was later tested in one of the prototypes.

The largest and heaviest heavy tank ever tested in the Soviet Union was the IS-7. It was fitted with a 130mm gun, and in spite of its weight was quite agile due to the use of a powerful naval diesel engine.

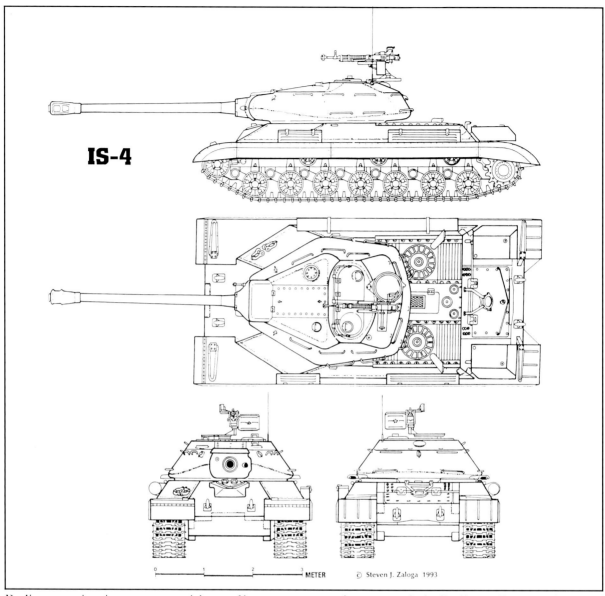

IS-4

© Steven J. Zaloga 1993

Berlin campaign is a controversial one. For many years, official Soviet accounts indicated that it did take part in the fighting. However, internal Soviet design histories that were restricted until recently deny that this was the case, and interviews with Soviet heavy tank designers also indicate that the IS-3 never saw combat action against Germany. Apparently, at least one regiment was rushed to Germany in April 1945, but hostilities ended before they were committed to the fighting. Other sources indicate that IS-3 heavy tanks were used in the August 1945 assault on the Japanese in Manchuria. The IS-3 was first publicly displayed at a victory parade in Berlin on 7 September 1945 which involved 52 IS-3 tanks from the 2nd Guards Tank Army.

The hull and turret configuration of the IS-3 were enormously influential for their sleek simplicity. In the Soviet Union, the shape was adopted on later Soviet medium tanks such as the T-54A, and has become standard until today's T-72B and T-80. In the West, the shape influenced designs such as the American M-48, German Leopard 1 and French AMX-30. Although influential overseas, the IS-3 had a troubled career in the post-war Soviet Army.

The design had been pushed into production much too quickly. Large numbers of IS-3 tanks were sidelined with mechanical problems. The welds on the thick armour plates on the front of the hull had a tendency to crack open, probably caused by the vibrations of rough cross-country travel and the shock of gun firing. From 1948-52, efforts were made to correct the problems. The changes to the design included strengthening the hull, improving the final drive, and reinforcing the engine mounts. Production of the IS-3 lasted until 1951 at Chelyabinsk, by which time about 1800 had been manufactured.

IS-4

While the IS-3 programme had been under way in 1944, the design team under L.S. Troyanov began work on a further elaboration of the IS-2 design under the codename Obiekt 701. Several alternatives were proposed on paper, and three designs were presented to the Red Army's tank directorate. These included the Obiekt 701-2, armed with the S-34 100mm gun; the Obiekt 701-5 with a different armour configuration; and the Obiekt 701-6 armed with the standard D-25T 122mm gun. The latter was accepted for further development. There were three significant changes in the Obiekt 701-6 design: thicker armour, a lengthened hull, and an uprated engine. The basic armour for the hull was increased to 160mm and the turret to 250mm. The 750 hp V-12 engine used a revised cooling system influenced by the layout of German Panther tanks, with the radiators under a pair of circular fans. The design was accepted for quantity production as the IS-4 tank in 1947.

After a short production run of only 200 tanks, IS-4 production was halted. The main criticism was that the speed and the mobility of the vehicle were inadequate. In the summer of 1950 after the outbreak of the Korean War, nearly all of the IS-4 regiments were shipped to the Far East. They were deployed to form the shock force for a tank army that Stalin was organising to intervene in the Korean conflict. In spite of intense pressure from the Chinese, Stalin decided against intervening in Korea for fear it would result in the outbreak of a

An IS-7 prototype is still preserved at the Kubinka armour museum. One of the stranger features of the IS-7 was the provision of

7.62mm machine guns in remotely controlled boxes on the hull side and the rear of the turret.

The IS-8 was basically an improved IS-3. The hull was lengthened to accommodate an improved powerplant with better cooling features. From a combat standpoint, its main

advantage was its much thicker armour. This IS-8 at the Kubinka museum shows the distinguishing feature of this version, the reliance on a simple telescopic sight for gunnery.

general war with the nuclear-armed American armed forces. The IS-4s remained in the region and in the late 1950s, they were modernised along the same lines as the IS-3M, remaining in service into the 1960s.

There have been repeated reports that several superheavy tanks were under development in the Soviet Union in 1945, including a 150 ton tank. However, none of these designs appear to have progressed beyond paper studies, or they remain so secret that they still are not discussed today. Among these designs were reputed to be the Vladimir Lenin VL-1, fitted with a front mounted engine and rear mounted turret.

POST WAR HISTORY

Both the IS-2 and IS-3 underwent modernisation programmes in the post-war years. In 1954, the IS-2s began to be rebuilt as the IS-2M. This programme included an increase in the amount of main gun ammunition from 28 to 35 rounds, an improved driver's periscope, the improved V-54K-IS engine, a modernized engine cooling and oil flow system, new radios and intercoms. Externally, the IS-2M had stowage increased by adding tool bins on the front hull side; dust skirts were also added. The parallel programme for the IS-3M began in 1960 and included additional hull reinforcement, replacement of the DShK 12.7mm machine gun with the DShKM, addition of a TVN-2 night vision device for the driver, substitution of the V-54K-IS engine, incorporation of the Mutlitsiklon air filter system, and many other small changes. New wheels were added from the T-10 heavy tank which had improved ball-bearings. In addition, external stowage was improved and dust skirts were added over the suspension. The IS-3M saw combat in Hungary in 1956 against the insurgent forces. A single heavy tank/assault gun regiment was committed to the fighting in central Budapest, and lost a number of IS-3M tanks and ISU-152K assault guns.

IS-6

In the immediate post-war years, the SKB-2 design bureau broke up into several competing

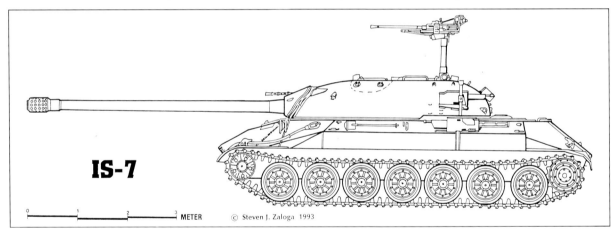

IS-7

0   1   2   3
                 METER   © Steven J. Zaloga 1993

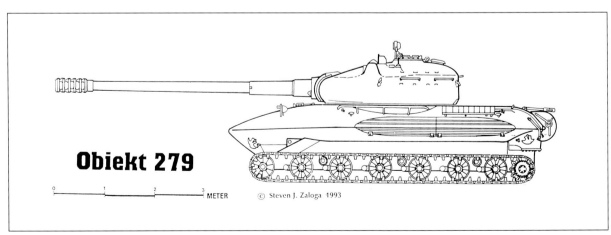

Obiekt 279

0   1   2   3
                 METER   © Steven J. Zaloga 1993

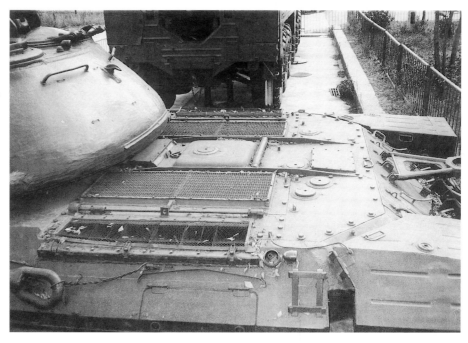

One of the main changes on the T-10 was a modification of the engine compartment which housed the V-12-5. The T-10M seen here used yet another modernised version of the engine, the V-12-6B with a 750 hp output.

design teams divided between the Chelyabinsk plant and the reopened Kirov Plant in Leningrad. No fewer than three separate design efforts were pursued. The main Kotin team was working on a project called Obiekt 703. The design used components from the IS-4 but the main focus of the design was to study the advantages of electrical transmissions. Electrical transmissions had significant theoretical advantages in transferring more usable power from the engine to the tracks, and also promised to offer improved steering and mobility. The concept had first been tried on the French St. Chamond tank in the First World War, and in the Second World War, the US Army tested the concept on the T-23 medium tank and the Germans fielded such a system on the Elefant tank destroyer. The Kotin team was undoubtedly most familiar with the German approach, as several Elefants had been captured at Kursk, and the NIIBT armoured research centre at Kubinka had done an extensive study of the transmission system. During the war years, a test-bed, called the IS-1E was built on a spare IS-1 chassis. The new transmission for the Obiekt 703 was based around a DK-305A 385 kilowatt generator. The Obiekt 703 was redesignated the IS-6, but the design never proved reliable enough for production. The

day of its first trials, the prototype burst into flames hardly 30 yards outside of the assembly hangar. It was soon found that the electrical transmission required too much cooling. The addition of sufficient fans added unacceptable weight to the design, as well as drawing off power. An attempt was made to retrieve the design by substituting the mechanical transmission from an IS-4. This vehicle was built as the izd.252, but offered no advantages over existing tanks and was cancelled.

IS-7

In the meantime, Nikolai Shashmurin's team had begun work on a completely new tank design, the IS-7, which bore no immediate connection to any previous Soviet heavy tank. The design was envisioned as a counterpart to the German Tiger II heavy tank in terms of armour and firepower. Shashmurin took advantage of the transfer back to Leningrad to examine a number of components developed by Soviet naval research institutes in the city. These included a 1050 hp marine diesel which would be needed to power such a heavy tank, and a 130mm gun derived from the naval 56-SM gun. The gun fired a huge 36.5 kg projectile at 945 m/s, which made it the most powerful weapon ever mounted in a Soviet tank up to that

The most characteristic feature of the T-10M was the new M-62 122mm gun with its multi-baffle muzzle brake. This version was fitted with full infra-red night fighting equipment and was the predominant version of this type.

point. The co-axial weapon was the powerful 14.5mm KPVT heavy machine gun, and no fewer than six other 7.62mm machine guns were provided, two co-axially in the mantlet, two on the right side of the hull, and two more on either side of the turret in small armoured barbettes. Another 14.5mm KPVT was fitted in a remote control mount on the roof for air defence. Given its thick armour, the IS-7 was the heaviest tank ever built in the Soviet Union, weighing 68 metric tons. In spite of its weight, its powerful engine gave it a higher road speed than previous Soviet heavy tanks.

The first prototype of the IS-7 was ready for testing in 1948. The crews were unhappy with the internal layout, which was extremely cramped even by Soviet standards. The ammunition was very heavy and this combined with the lack of space in the vehicle made it difficult to load the main armament. The number of machine guns was considered excessive, and the location of the

With the withdrawal of the T-10M from service in the 1970s, its components were put to other uses. Here a T-10M turret has been used to arm an armoured train.

The most common use for worn-out T-10s was emplacement as static defensive pillboxes along the Chinese frontier.

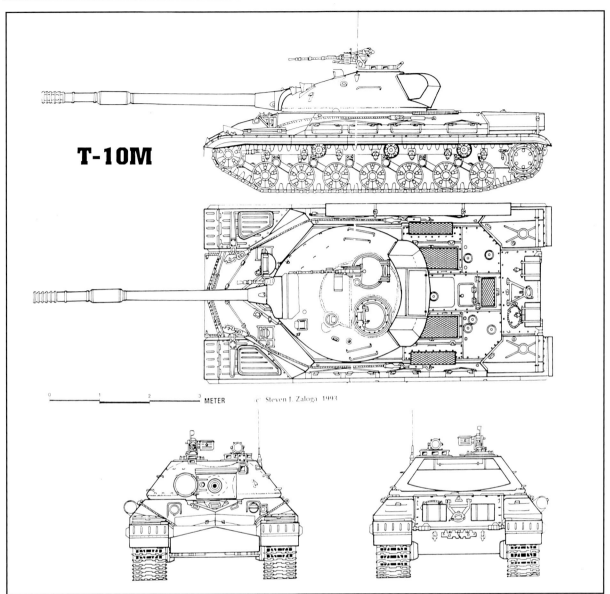

T-10M

0   1   2   3   METER   © Steven J. Zaloga 1993

ammunition trays made it impossible to reload these weapons in combat. The suspension used internal shock absorbers in the wheels patterned after those on the German Tiger II. Unfortunately, these were subject to rapid wear and led to breakdowns when the tank was operated near its top speed. The Soviet Army's armoured vehicle directorate was very unhappy about the vehicle's weight for two reasons. Firstly, the extreme weight would tax the limited Soviet road and rail network and the tank would be very difficult to employ tactically since there were few bridges that would withstand its weight. Secondly, heavy weight implied high cost, both in the purchase price and in regular operations and maintenance. In the end, only a small series of test vehicles were manufactured. The IS-7 remains the heaviest tank ever built in the USSR. In some respects it was ahead of its time. The level of firepower and armour on the IS-7 was very similar to that found on NATO tanks in the 1960s, such as the US Army M-60A1 or the British Chieftain. On the other hand, its main gun and fire controls suffered from the constraints imposed by 1940s technology. These limitations also denied them the accuracy of later tank guns.

The ultimate evolution of the T-10 series was the Obiekt 277. This version used a new cast bow, an enlarged turret with 130mm gun, and a lengthened hull. It never entered production owing to Khrushchev's unhappiness with the heavy tank concept.

Undoubtedly the strangest Soviet heavy tank was the Obiekt 279. This tank used a very unusual hull configuration with four tracks to permit it to survive the nearby detonation of a tactical nuclear weapon. It proved too complicated and expensive for mass production.

A rear view of the unusual Obiekt 279. The outer panels of the hull were hinged to allow them to swing down and out of the way during rail transport. At the rear of the vehicle are a pair of supplementary external fuel tanks.

IS-8

The experimental heavy tanks of the 1940s helped the Soviet Army define more clearly what it sought in a heavy tank design. In the end, weight and cost constraints led to the conclusion that an updated IS-3 design would satisfy these needs. As a result, development of the IS-8 began in 1948. The IS-8 used components from many of the experimental tanks. For example, the electrical turret traverse and elevation were derived from the IS-7, as was the short torsion bar suspension. The V-12-5 engine was a derivative of the type used in the IS-4 and IS-6, and the track also came from the IS-4. The D-25TA gun was a slightly improved version of the same gun used on the IS-2 and IS-3. The new BR-472 ballistic-capped 122mm projectile was introduced which offered better penetration than the BR-417B projectile. The turret resembled the IS-3 turret, but the basic armour was raised to 200mm. Engine cooling was improved by boosting the airflow through the radiators using exhaust gases. The added weight of the IS-8 as well as the improved engine cooling system led to a lengthened hull which had an additional set of road wheels similar to the IS-4. Production of the IS-8 began in late 1950 or early 1951 at Chelyabinsk. There are also some reports that indicate that production may have taken place at the tank plant in Omsk as well.

T-10

Following Stalin's death in 1953, the IS-8 was redesignated the T-10 as part of the de-Stalinisation programme. As the pace of T-10 production increased during the early 1950s, additional improvements were added. The T-10A version incorporated the new D-25TS gun which had a stabilisation system added in the vertical axis, as well as a bore evacuator. One of the main problems of the Soviet heavy tanks had been the heavy weight of the projectiles. As a result, the T-10A

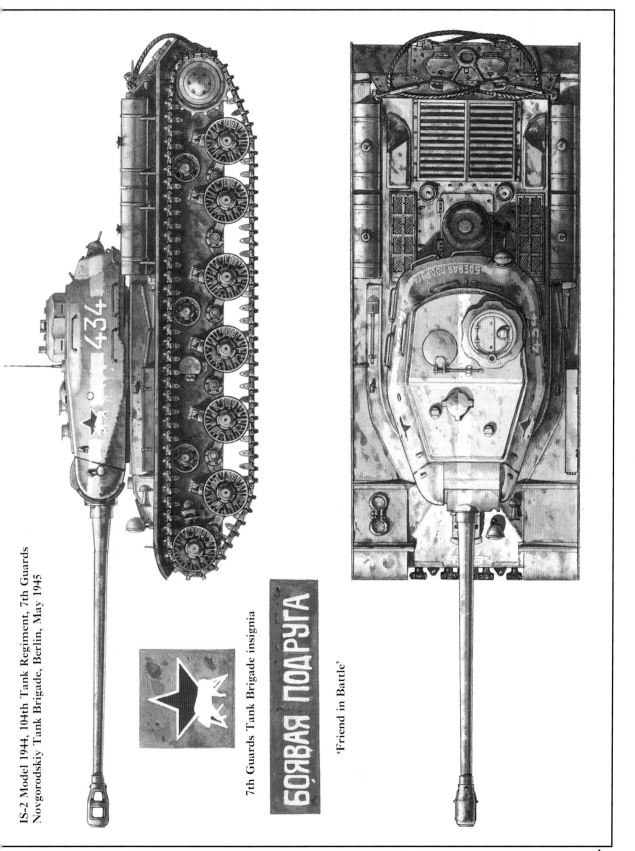

IS-2 Model 1944, 104th Tank Regiment, 7th Guards
Novgorodskiy Tank Brigade, Berlin, May 1945

7th Guards Tank Brigade insignia

БОЯВАЯ ПОДРУГА

'Friend in Battle'

A

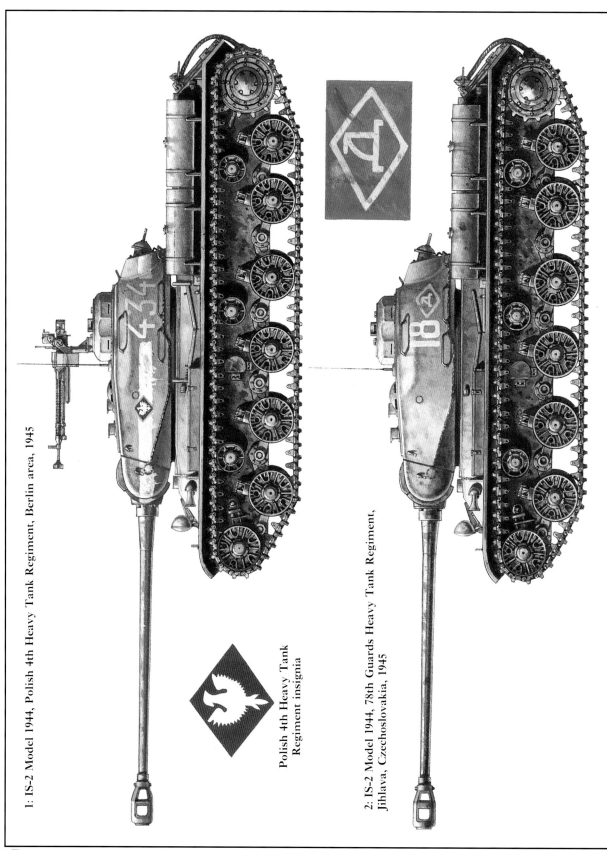

1: IS-2 Model 1944, Polish 4th Heavy Tank Regiment, Berlin area, 1945

Polish 4th Heavy Tank
Regiment insignia

2: IS-2 Model 1944, 78th Guards Heavy Tank Regiment,
Jihlava, Czechoslovakia, 1945

B

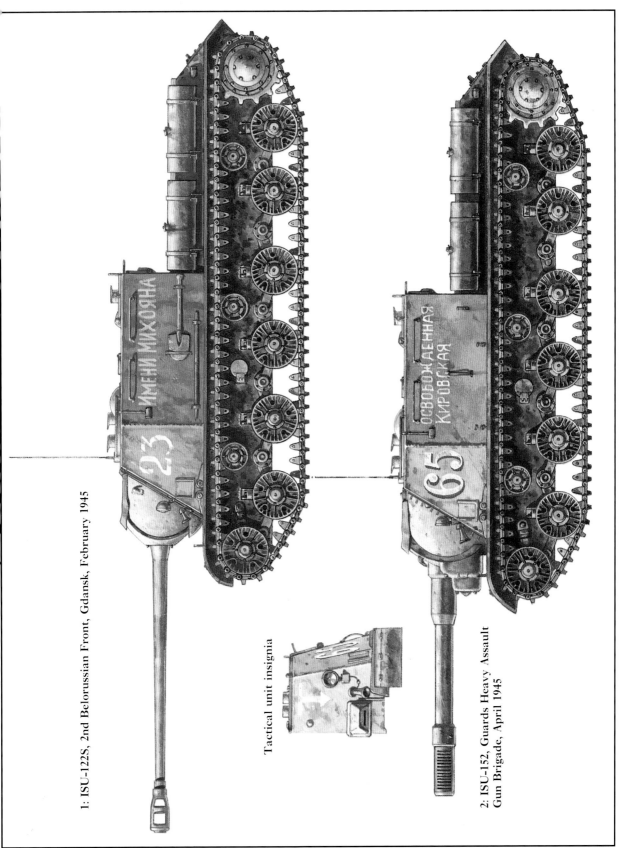

1: ISU-122S, 2nd Belorussian Front, Gdansk, February 1945

Tactical unit insignia

2: ISU-152, Guards Heavy Assault Gun Brigade, April 1945

C

IS-2 Model 1944
95th Guards Independent Heavy Tank Regiment, Berlin, 1945

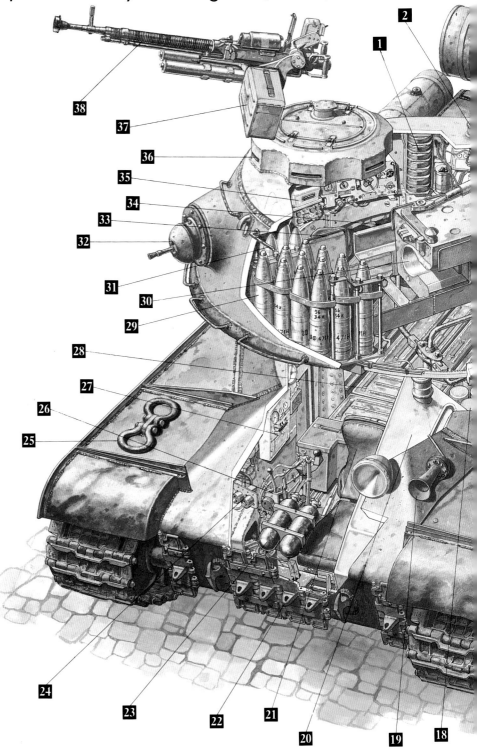

KEY

1. Spare DT7 7.62mm machine gun drums
2. Gunner's PT-4-17 periscopic sight
3. Gunner's 10-T-17 telescopic sight
4. D-25T gun recuperator assembly
5. co-axial DT 7.62mm machine gun
6. Engine radiator grills
7. Towing cables
8. Jettisonable 200 litre fuel drums
9. D-25T Model 1943 122mm tank gun
10. External 75 litre fuel tanks
11. Electrical conduit to turret
12. Vehicle tools (wood saw)
13. Vehicle black-out light
14. Floor ammunition stowage boxes
15. Loader's seat
16. Spare DT 7.62mm ammunition drums
17. ZIP tool stowage bin
18. Propellant cases for 122mm projectiles
19. Vehicle claxon
20. Forward vehicle fuel stowage
21. Driver's seat
22. Spare track links
23. Compressed air bottles for starting engine
24. Driver's instruments
25. Towing shackles
26. Driver's controls (clutch and braking lever)
27. Driver's instruments
28. Floor ammunition stowage bins
29. OF-471N 122mm projectiles (HE-Frag)
30. D-25T 122m gun breach
31. BR-471B 122mm projectiles (AP-T)
32. DT 7.62mm close defence machine gun
33. Commander's station
34. Gunner's station
35. Vehicular 10RK radio transceiver
36. Commander's cupola
37. Ammunition box for DShK machine gun
38. DshK Model 1938 12.7mm machine gun

D

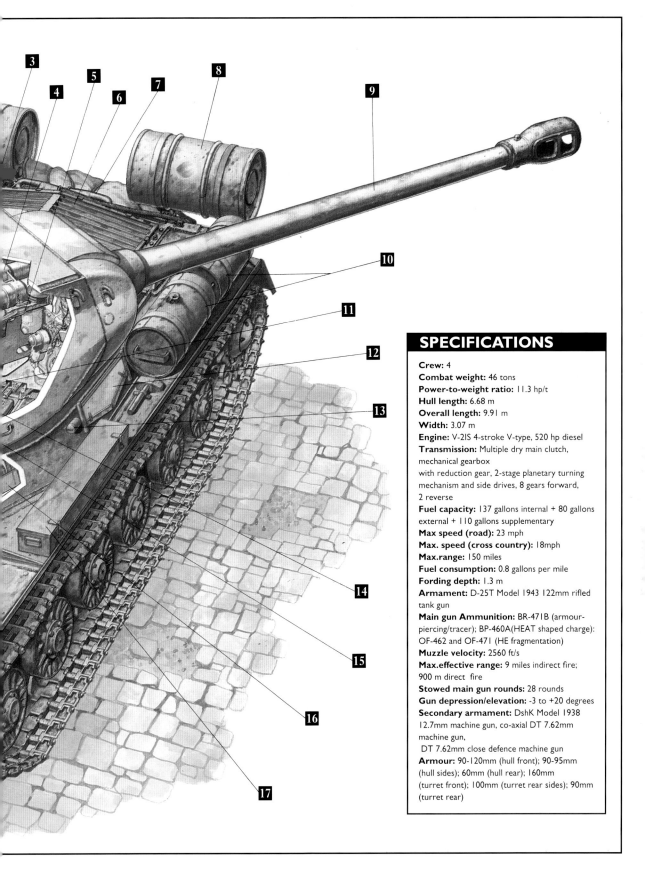

SPECIFICATIONS

Crew: 4
Combat weight: 46 tons
Power-to-weight ratio: 11.3 hp/t
Hull length: 6.68 m
Overall length: 9.91 m
Width: 3.07 m
Engine: V-2IS 4-stroke V-type, 520 hp diesel
Transmission: Multiple dry main clutch, mechanical gearbox
with reduction gear, 2-stage planetary turning mechanism and side drives, 8 gears forward, 2 reverse
Fuel capacity: 137 gallons internal + 80 gallons external + 110 gallons supplementary
Max speed (road): 23 mph
Max. speed (cross country): 18mph
Max.range: 150 miles
Fuel consumption: 0.8 gallons per mile
Fording depth: 1.3 m
Armament: D-25T Model 1943 122mm rifled tank gun
Main gun Ammunition: BR-471B (armour-piercing/tracer); BP-460A(HEAT shaped charge): OF-462 and OF-471 (HE fragmentation)
Muzzle velocity: 2560 ft/s
Max.effective range: 9 miles indirect fire; 900 m direct fire
Stowed main gun rounds: 28 rounds
Gun depression/elevation: -3 to +20 degrees
Secondary armament: DshK Model 1938 12.7mm machine gun, co-axial DT 7.62mm machine gun,
 DT 7.62mm close defence machine gun
Armour: 90-120mm (hull front); 90-95mm (hull sides); 60mm (hull rear); 160mm (turret front); 100mm (turret rear sides); 90mm (turret rear)

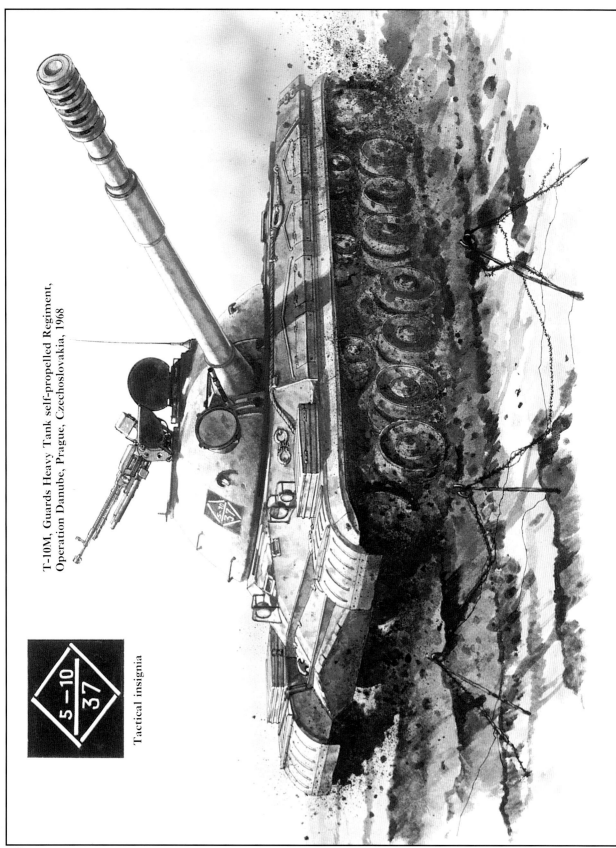

T-10M, Guards Heavy Tank self-propelled Regiment, Operation Danube, Prague, Czechoslovakia, 1968

Tactical insignia

E

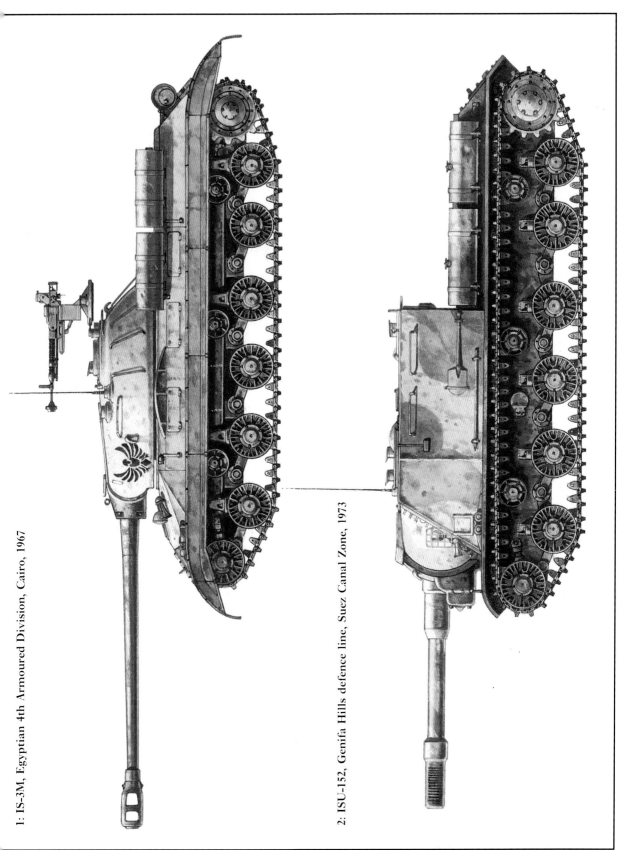

1: IS-3M, Egyptian 4th Armoured Division, Cairo, 1967

2: ISU-152, Genifa Hills defence line, Suez Canal Zone, 1973

F

IS–3, Coastal Defence Unit, Kurile Islands, 1992

G

Widely regarded as the best Soviet heavy tank was Isakov's Obiekt 770. This very modern design was comparable in size and weight to the US Army's M60A1 tank, but better armed. Due to Khrushchev's disfavour with heavy tanks, it never entered production. Isakov later went on to fame and fortune as the designer of the BMP infantry combat vehicles.

added a simple rammer. The gunner loaded the projectile and casing on a special tray, and the rammer pushed them into the breech. On the T-10A, the TSh-2-27 sight was replaced by a new TPS-1 periscopic sight and a TUP telescopic sight. Other improvements on the T-10A included a TVN-1 night vision device for the gunner and a GPK-48 gyrocompass. In the mid 1950s, this was followed by the T-10B. This version added a two-axis stabilisation system for the gun and new T2S-29 fire control sights but externally was very similar to the T-10A. The final variant of the series, the T-10M, was introduced in 1957. The most important change was the addition of the longer M-62-TS gun, which had better armour penetration than the earlier D-25, about 185mm at 1,000 metres (160mm for the D-25) using the normal armour piercing round. In addition, the gun could fire the BP-460A HEAT projectile which offered penetration of about 300mm. The M-62-TS gun was fitted with the Liven two-axis stabilization system and could be easily distinguished by its distinctive multi-slotted muzzle brake. The T-10M version also substituted KPVT 14.5mm heavy machine guns for both the 12.7 DShK co-axial and anti-aircraft machine guns. The KPVT was a closer ballistic match for the

new M-62 gun, and so could be used for rough ranging. The T-10M used the uprated 750 hp V-12-6 engine. By the time that production ended in 1962, about 8000 T-10s of all versions had been manufactured, making it, numerically, the most significant tank of the Stalin series.

Post-war Soviet heavy tank organisation

In the post-war years, Soviet heavy tank units underwent several reorganisations. During the 1947 reorganization of the mechanised forces, a composite regiment was added to each tank or mechanized division. The US Army called these composite regiments 'heavy tank/assault gun regiments', but the actual Russian name is not certain. These regiments contained 44-46 heavy tanks and 21 heavy assault guns of either the ISU-122 or ISU-152 types. The composite regiment was intended to provide additional firepower to the division, particularly in breakthrough operations.

With the production of the T-10 in full swing, the Soviet Army began experimenting with heavy tank divisions. These divisions were organised like conventional tank divisions, but had two heavy and one medium tank regiment, instead of the three medium tank regiments in a normal division. Two of these divisions, the 13th and 25th Guards

The ISU-152 assault gun was widely used in the final year of the Second World War to provide mobile fire support during breakthrough operations. Here the crew consults a local officer while trying to get directions in the Polish town of Czestochowa during the January 1945 winter fighting.

Heavy Tank Divisions, served in the Group of Soviet Forces-Germany in the 1950s and 1960s. It is believed that a further two or three of these divisions existed, at least one in the Far East. These divisions were intended to act as the shock forces of the tank armies during offensive operations. During the 1958-59 reorganisation, the composite heavy tank/assault gun regiment was replaced by a homogenous heavy tank regiment. These were a formidable formation, equipped with 100 IS-3M or T-10 tanks.

In the early 1960s, the T-10s underwent a factory rebuild to improve their transmission. A new six speed transmission and main clutch were installed in all the vehicles.

Post-war adversaries

The thick armour of the IS-3 and T-10 tanks caused considerable consternation in both the US Army and the British Army. This led both armies to develop their own countermeasures. The British result was the Conqueror which entered service in 1956, and in the USA the M-103 which entered service in 1958. Both were armed with very long 120mm guns with substantial armour penetration. The M-103 could penetrate 221mm of armour at 30° at 1,000 yards, and 196mm at 2000 yards using armour piercing

ammunition. Using HEAT projectiles it could penetrate 330mm of armour at 2,000 yards. Both vehicles were heavier than their Soviet counterparts, the Conqueror at 65 tons, and the M-103 at 62 tons.

Had there been a conflict between NATO and the Warsaw Pact in the late 1950s, the tactical balance would not have been all that dissimilar from the German-Soviet fighting of 1944. NATO tanks of the late 1950s, such as the US Army M-48, would have had a tough time dealing with the T-10 frontally at ranges of 1,000 metres, much as the Panther had difficulty with IS-2s in 1944. The new HEAT (High-explosive anti-tank) ammunition used with the M-48's 90mm gun could not penetrate the thickest sections of the T-10's armour. The M-48 could only have penetrated the side of the vehicle. The T-10's 122mm gun could penetrate nearly any NATO medium tank of the period from 1,000 metres. In a duel between the T-10 and NATO heavy tanks such as the Conqueror and M-103, the NATO tanks would have had a modest advantage. The M-103 and Conqueror had sophisticated coincidence rangefinders that offered excellent accuracy at long ranges in the hands of a well trained crew. The T-10 relied on a stadiameric rangefinder which was not particularly efficient at ranges greater than 1,000 metres. The HEAT projectile fired by the M-103

The interior of the ISU-152 is relatively spacious until you realise that five crewmen plus ammunition must fit in here. To the right is the breech of the ML-20S 152mm howitzer, while towards the centre is the driver's station.

could penetrate the T-10 frontally, and its shaped charge warhead had the same penetration regardless of range. The Soviets never deployed a heavy tank with the type of elaborate fire controls found on the NATO vehicles. However, the next generation main battle tank, the T-64 did use one.

By the 1960s, the T-10s armour advantage had disappeared. New NATO main battle tanks such as the M60A1 and Chieftain had comparable protection and their 105 and 120mm guns could penetrate the T-10's frontal armour at standard combat ranges.

Later heavy tank designs

Although the T-10 was the last of Soviet heavy tank in series production, other heavy tank designs did follow it. The Soviet Army decided to continue to pursue heavy tank development even after the service introduction of the IS-8. Around 1955, a dual programme was begun to examine alternative heavy tanks for the future – the Obiekt 277 and Obiekt 279. The main feature shared in common was an advanced version of the 130mm gun developed for the ill-fated IS-7 heavy tank, mated to optical rangefinders for greater long-range accuracy. The new turret included an ammunition assist system for the loader, and was fitted with infra-red night fighting equipment as

well. Both tanks would share a very similar turret design. However, the hull of both tanks was significantly different. The Obiekt 277 used a modernised hull evolved out of the T-10 chassis, but lengthened with an additional set of road wheels. The team headed by L.S. Troyanov, however, came up with a far more radical approach.

Troyanov's Obiekt 279 was designed to fight on the nuclear battlefield. Beginning in 1953, the Soviet Army had participated in a number of nuclear tests, placing several tank designs in the blast area. In September 1954, a special atomic bomb test was conducted in the Totskoye region with selected army units taking part. It became evident at the tests that tanks near the nuclear blast area were often knocked over by the shock waves that ensued. Although overturned, the tanks were intact and still functional. This led to the requirement for a tank that could survive a nearby explosion of a tactical nuclear weapon. Troyanov's approach to the requirement was to increase the surface area of the track and reduce the centre of gravity. In addition, the hull would be aerodynamically shaped to withstand the high speed wind that accompanied the blast's shock wave as well as to reduce radiation effects to the crew inside. The vehicle was fitted with hydropneumatic suspension

The ISU-122 and ISU-152 were virtually identical except for the substitution of an A-19S 122mm gun tube in the ISU-122 version. This Polish ISU-122 was preserved at Poznan. (Janusz Magnuski)

so that the entire chassis could be lowered closer to the ground to further resist overturning.

The prototype of the Obiekt 279 was completed in 1957. It had a remarkable appearance. The suspension was modular with four sets of running gear. Each pair of running gear were attached to a central core which also served as the main fuel supply. The hull was oval in shape when viewed from above, with very steeply angled sides. The hull configuration permitted a great deal of dead space that could be used to contain anti-radiation material. It was powered by a 1,000 hp, 12 cylinder diesel engine which gave it excellent mobility for a 60 ton tank, and was capable of speeds of up to 35 mph. The turret and armament of the Obiekt 279 were essentially similar to those on the Obiekt 277, with a 130mm gun mounted in a large, conventional 3-man turret, with a coincidence range-finder. The tests on the tank were successful in view of the novelty of the design. But the hull construction made the tank extremely expensive to produce and it was never accepted for service.

The final heavy tank developed in the USSR was the product of a new design team, headed by an unknown young designer at Chelyabinsk named Pavel Isakov. The experimental tank, labelled the Obiekt 770, attempted to incorporate the heavy armour and heavy firepower of the 1950s tanks in a more compact and lighter design.

The ISU-122S, also called the ISU-122-2, used the improved D-25S 122mm gun which had a tank-type breech. While this was being incorporated in the design, a new ball-shaped mantlet was also developed which provided a wider angle of traverse for the gun.

The prototype was completed in 1957 and sent to state trials. Although it was widely regarded to be a success, its future was doomed from the start due to political developments in Moscow.

By the mid 1950s, Nikita Khrushchev had emerged as Stalin's heir. Khrushchev was faced by many of the same problems as Gorbachev in the 1980s, namely a bloated military and a stagnant economy. Khrushchev was determined to solve both problems in a related fashion. Major cuts for the armed forces were planned, both in manpower and equipment. The Soviet Union would change its strategic concepts of defence, and place more emphasis on strategic nuclear-armed missiles, with less emphasis on the conventional forces. The heavy tank in particular was viewed by Khrushchev as evidence of the 'old-thinking' and in 1960, he ordered heavy tank production to be terminated.

In fact, Khrushchev's order was not as rash as it might seem. The Soviet heavy tank, at least so far as the T-10 family was concerned, was nearing the end of its evolutionary potential. Its main gun was impressive by Second World War standards, but in the late 1950s, Petrov's design bureau in Perm had developed advanced smooth-bore cannon for medium tanks that had superior

The ISU-152 Model 1945 was an attempt to develop an assault gun version of the IS-3 tank. Although the ballistic shape of the hull was superior to the standard ISU-152, it was not accepted for production.

performance. Moreover, these new guns could be incorporated into a 35 ton medium tank chassis. The Morozov Design Bureau in Kharkov was working on just such a tank, the Obiekt 430, which would emerge in 1965 as the T-64. These advanced new tanks were dubbed *osnovnoi* tank, standard tank, a concept first broached in 1942 with the KV-13 universal tank. Instead of medium tanks and heavy tanks, a single type could be fielded which would fulfil both roles. The reformers argued that the long-range fire support was better left to new missile armed tank destroyers.

Heavy tanks did not immediately disappear from the Soviet Army. The heavy tank division remained in service until 1969 when one of the two heavy tank regiments in the division were replaced with medium tanks. Finally, in 1970, the heavy tank divisions disappeared and the separate heavy tank regiments were gradually disbanded. But as late as 1978, there were still about 2,300 heavy tanks in service, mainly in the Far East. Most of the heavy tanks were not actually melted down, but merely withdrawn into inactive reserves.

Soviet heavy tanks today

Some heavy tanks remain in service to this day, though not in a mechanised role. Due to tensions

with China in the early 1960s, border defences were substantially beefed up. One manner of doing this was to add pillboxes along the frontier. One of the most cost-effective approaches was to bury outdated tanks as improvised pillboxes, with only their turrets showing. This was first done with IS-2 and IS-3 tanks but in the 1970s the process was extended to the T-10. Many, if not most, of these tank pillboxes remain in place to this day.

The final heavy assault gun developed in the Soviet Union was the Obiekt 268, which mated a modified ML-20S 152mm howitzer with the T-10 hull.

Rangefinding was provided by a stereoscopic rangefinder on the right forward cupola on the roof. This type was not accepted for production.

As the ISU-152 and ISU-122 were withdrawn from service in the 1960s, they were often converted into BTT-1 heavy armoured recovery vehicles. The main gun was removed, the opening plated over, and other features more appropriate to the recovery role were added. This is a BTT-1 captured by the Israeli Army after the 1973 Sinai fighting.

STALIN TANKS IN FOREIGN SERVICE

The Stalin tanks were never widely exported. During the Second World War, two allied armies were provided with IS-2 tanks, although the post-war years saw a more widespread market develop.

Poland
The Polish People's Army (LWP) received 71 IS-2 tanks which were used to form two heavy tank regiments, the 4th and 5th Heavy Tank Regiments (*Pulk ciezkich czolgow*). Both regiments saw extensive fighting from the winter 1944-45 offensive through to the final assaults on Berlin. The 4th Heavy Tank Regiment was committed to action in Pomerania during the January 1945 offensive, and by the war's end was credited with 31 German armoured vehicles and 76 artillery pieces destroyed in combat, for a loss of 14 IS-2 heavy tanks. The 5th Heavy Tank Regiment went into action in the final month of the war, seeing action in the Berlin and Prague campaigns. Two other regiments, the 6th and 7th, were not completely organised by the time the fighting ceased. At the end of the war, the Polish LWP had 26 IS-2 tanks still in service, having returned 21 to the Red Army and having lost 24 in combat or to mechanical problems. These remaining tanks formed the post-war 7th Heavy Tank Regiment. Poland received two IS-3 Stalin tanks for trials in 1946, but never adopted this type for service use.

Czechoslovakia
The Czechoslovak Army, formed in the Soviet Union, fielded the 1st Tank Brigade and was equipped mainly with the T-34 and T-34/85 tanks. In the final days of the war, the brigade was provided with a small number of IS-2 tanks to take part in victory celebrations in Prague. But these were not a standard part of the equipment of the Czechoslovak Army. As in the Polish case, the Czechoslovak People's Army was sold at least one IS-3 tank for trials purposes after the war. No Warsaw Pact army deployed the IS-3 in their tank units, nor did any attempt to acquire the more modern T-10 heavy tank.

China
IS-2 heavy tanks were exported to the People's Republic of China in small numbers in the early 1950s. Several Chinese accounts of the Korean War have suggested that they were committed to the fighting against UN forces in Korea in 1951-53, but there has never been any evidence that they were encountered by the US Army or other UN forces. US intelligence reports indicate that after the war, the Chinese Army in Korea had four independent GHQ armoured regiments each organised with four T-34/85 companies, and a single IS-2 company with five tanks each. The Chinese IS-2 forces, though probably small in number, had influence far beyond their actual combat capabilities. During the Indochina War of the 1950s, the French Army was deeply concerned that China would intervene in northern Vietnam with the IS-2 tanks. As a result, at least one Panther tank was shipped to Indochina on an experimental basis as a possible counterweight to the Stalin tank threat. In the end the tank broke down and the French dispatched American M-36 90mm tank destroyers instead.

Cuba and North Korea

Cuba received about two regiments of IS-2 heavy tanks in the early 1960s. There have been reports that these vehicles were still operational in the 1980s. North Korea was supplied with both IS-2 and IS-3 tanks, mainly the latter. During the 1960s, its two armoured divisions each had a single regiment of heavy tanks.

The Middle East

The most extensive post-war combat use of the IS-3 tanks came in the 1960s. The Egyptian Army acquired about 100 IS-3M tanks from the USSR as part of its modernisation programme. During the 1967 Six Day War, one regiment with 21 IS-3Ms was stationed with the 7th Infantry Division at Rafah, and the 125th Tank Brigade of the 6th Mechanized Division at Kuntilla was also

Components from Stalin heavy tanks were used on many different projects. In the mid-1950s, the Kotin design bureau at the Kirov Plant in Leningrad designed several super-heavy self-propelled artillery vehicles

for firing nuclear projectiles. This particular example is the Kondensator 2P self-propelled gun, armed with the Grabin SM-54 406mm gun. It had a range of 28 km with a 470 kg projectile.

equipped with about 60 IS-3Ms. The IS-3M was the most feared tank in Egyptian service due to its thick armour. Israeli infantry units and paratrooper units had considerable difficulty when the Stalins were encountered, as the existing bazookas and other anti-tank weapons could not penetrate its frontal armour. Many Israeli tanks, especially the various models of Shermans, also had problems. Even the more modern tanks, such as the M-48A2 Patton with its 90mm gun, could not easily penetrate its armour at normal battle ranges. There were a number of engagements between M-48A2 Pattons of the 7th Armoured Brigade and IS-3M regiment supporting the Egyptian positions near Rafah, with several Pattons being knocked out in the fighting. The Israeli tankers were usually able to overcome the armour problem by better training and tactics. The Egyptian tanks were most dangerous when firing from ambush positions. In battle against other tanks the slow rate of fire of the Stalin and its rudimentary fire controls proved to be a problem. In total, the Egyptian Army lost 73 IS-3Ms in the 1967 war. At least one regiment of IS-3M tanks was still in Egyptian Army service during the 1973 Yom Kippur War, but does not appear to have seen much fighting. The Israeli

Army put a small number of captured IS-3M tanks into service for a short time in the late 1960s. The tank was not popular in service, its engine being poorly suited to the hot climate. In an attempt to extend the life of these tanks, Israeli tank depots removed the V-54-IS engine, and replaced it with a complete powerpack from a T-54A tank, including the engine deck. This did little good, and after the 1973 war, the Israeli Army dug in most of the surviving IS-3 tanks in the Jordan river area and used them as defensive pillboxes.

VARIANTS

The most important variants of the Stalin heavy tanks were the associated heavy assault guns. In fact, during the Second World War, more heavy assault guns were built on the IS-2 chassis than the basic heavy tank variants. This was in part due to the greater economy of a heavy assault gun compared to a heavy tank. It was also due to the fact that in the overwatch role, a common tactic with both heavy tanks and heavy assault guns, a turret was not absolutely essential.

Heavy assault guns

The first heavy assault guns were the SU-152, built on the KV-1S chassis. About 700 of these were completed from April to September 1943 at Chelyabinsk. They saw extensive combat use during the battle of Kursk in the summer of 1943, where the earned they nickname *Zvierboi* (animal hunter), for their ability to destroy the heavy new Tiger I tanks and Elefant tank destroyers. In fact, at the time, they were the only Soviet armoured vehicle capable of regularly defeating the new German heavy AFVs.

The success of the SU-152 made it inevitable that similar vehicles would be built on the new IS heavy tank chassis when it entered production at Chelyabinsk. Work on the izd.241 prototype took place in parallel to the prototype for the IS-85. It resembled the SU-152, although the superstructure sides gave it a higher appearance. Actually, the KV hull was deeper than the IS hull, so this

required the superstructure on the izd.241 to be higher to accommodate the gun and ammunition. The internal volume of both vehicles was about the same, and both carried 20 rounds of ammunition. The weapon on the izd.241 was the same ML-20S 152mm gun-howitzer as on the SU-152. The prototype of the izd.241 was demonstrated to the GKO in the summer of 1943 and it was accepted for production as the ISU-152.

The main problem encountered in the production of this vehicle was the shortage of ML-20 barrels. The Soviet artillery factories were having a hard time keeping up with the demand for these weapons. However, there was surplus capacity for the A-19 122mm gun as well as for its ammunition. As a result, in the summer of 1943, the GKO ordered the SKB-2 design bureau at Chelyabinsk to examine the possibility of fitting the A-19 to the ISU-152 hull. This was not a major problem, as both the A-19 and ML-20 were fitted to the same carriage in their normal towed artillery versions. The only major adaptation required was in the internal ammunition stowage. A prototype of this vehicle, the izd.242, was completed later in 1943. It was accepted for production by the GKO as the ISU-122. The first 35 ISU-122 and ISU-152 were completed in December 1943 alongside IS-85 production.

The formation of the first ISU-122 and ISU-152 units took place in February 1944. They were organised much the same as the new heavy tanks, in special regiments called separate heavy self-propelled artillery regiments (OTSAP: *otdelniy tyazheliy samokhodno-artilleriskiy polk*) with 21 assault guns in four batteries. Generally, the regiments were homogenous, that is, equipped entirely with ISU-122 or ISU-152, not a mixture of types. No distinction was made between the two types so far as deployment was concerned. By the end of the war, a total of 53 of these regiments were formed.

The tactics of the assault gun regiments were not significantly different from those of the heavy tanks regiments. Their main role was to support offensive breakthrough operations and they were generally reserved at army or front level for these tasks. They were expected to deal with German

The Stalin heavy tank chassis was also used on a variety of missile launcher vehicles. This is an early unguided nuclear rocket system, possibly designated Mars, which was called FROG-1 by NATO.

strongpoints and anti-tank defences from long range, and provide overwatch firepower during infantry and tank attacks. They were not intended for close-range engagements, since the limited traverse of their main guns made them vulnerable to side attack. The ISU-122 was especially popular as a long range tank destroyer. These were commonly used in ambush situations when German heavy tanks were encountered. The ISU-152 was far less suited to tank fighting. The 152mm ML-20S gun-howitzer had mediocre anti-armour performance compared to the 122mm gun due to the slow muzzle velocity of its massive shell. It could penetrate 120mm of armour at 1,000 metres compared to 160mm for the 122mm gun. In addition, its fire controls did not make it well suited to engagements beyond 1,000 metres. As a result, the ISU-152 was generally used in missions where its excellent high-explosive firepower could be used to best advantage. It was particularly popular in urban fighting where its howitzer could devastate entrenched German positions.

The first major commitment of the new assault guns came in the summer of 1944 during Operation Bagration. This was the largest concentration of heavy armour to date, with no fewer than 14 Guards assault gun regiments assigned to the breakthrough. The heaviest concentrations were three regiments with 5th Army and two with 49th Army, both part of a double pronged assault on the Belorussian capital of Minsk. The assault gun regiments particularly distinguished themselves in the fighting at Polotsk and Vitebsk. Eight of the regiments were honoured by having liberated cities added to their unit name, three received the Order of the Red Banner and three the Order of the Red Star. The ISU-122 and ISU-152 soon earned the reputation of being the deadliest enemy of the dreaded German Tiger I tanks. The reputation was well deserved, for example, of the 12 Tiger I tanks of s.Pz.Abt. 502 destroyed in the summer 1944 fighting in Belorussia and the Baltic coast, about half could be attributed to ISU-122s or ISU-152s.

Various efforts were made to improve the firepower of the ISUs during 1944. The A-19 122mm gun had been specially modified for use on the IS-2 tank with a semi-automatic drop breech. This variant of the gun, designated D-25T, increased the rate of fire from about two rounds per minute to three or four rounds per minute. As a result, it was decided to adapt this weapon to the ISU-122 as well. An experimental mounting for the weapon was fitted to the izd.249

prototype. Besides the new gun, the izd.249 also incorporated a modernized mantlet which permitted greater traverse of the gun. This was accepted for production as the ISU-122S, although it was also called the ISU-122-2.

Following the appearance of the Panther and Tiger I tanks in 1943, the Soviets expected a heavier German armoured vehicle to appear in 1944. As a result, a variety of attempts were made to improve the anti-armour performance of the 152mm gun-howitzer on the ISU-152, as well as to develop new weapons that could cope with any larger German tank. There were at least four programmes, under the project names izd.243, 246, 247, and 250. The ISU-152-1 examined the long barrelled BL-8 152mm gun on the ISU-152 chassis. This weapon increased the muzzle velocity to 900 m/s which substantially improved the anti-armour penetration of the ISU-152. The related ISU-152-2 examined a slightly different gun, the BL-10, which offered similar performance. The ISU-130 mounted the S-26 130mm gun, an adaptation of a standard naval gun. The main advantage of this weapon over the improved 152mm guns was that the ammunition was less bulky, so 25 rounds could be carried instead of the usual 21. A modified version of this gun, the

S-26-1, was also mounted in an ISU-122S chassis, the ISU-122BM. The S-26-1 130mm gun had a lengthened barrel which increased its muzzle velocity to 1,000 m/s and improved its anti-armour performance accordingly.

None of these improved assault guns were accepted for production. By the time that their testing was completed, the ISU-122 and ISU-152 had already proved successful in combat, and the new German Tiger II heavy tank was never seen in significant numbers. The final assault gun project of the war was ISU-152 Model 1945, an attempt to build a new 152mm assault gun on the chassis of the new IS-3 tank. It used a much more angled superstructure than the ISU-152 based on the IS-2 chassis, but in reality offered little other advantage. It was decided to stay with the ISU-152 as the standard Soviet heavy assault gun. In March 1945, production of the ISU-152 shifted to the old Kirov Plant in Leningrad as part of the effort to rebuild the city's industrial base after the horrific 900 day siege. ISU production in 1944 totalled 2,510 vehicles, plus an additional 1,530 up to June 1945. This meant that total wartime ISU production totalled about 4075 vehicles. ISU-152 production lasted until 1955, and total post-war ISU-152 production totalled about 2,450 vehicles.

Production of the ISU-122 was halted shortly after the war, but restarted in 1947. From 1947 to 1952, about 3130 ISU-122s were manufactured.

During the post-war years, the ISU-152 underwent two major modernisation efforts. In 1956, the ISU-152s began to be modernised as the ISU-152K. A new commander's cupola was introduced with the TPKU designator sight, and a ring for the 12.7mm DShK anti-aircraft machine gun was also added. Internal ammunition stowage was increased to 30 rounds for the main gun. An improved PS-10 telescopic sight was substituted. A V-54K engine replaced the earlier diesel, and external fuel tank stowage was increased from three to six cylindrical tanks. The engine cooling system was also improved and new radios were introduced. The ISU-152K became the standard post-war version of this heavy assault gun. In 1959, a second set of improvements were added on the final ISU-152M series. This basically paralleled the post-war IS-2M modernisation programme and included such features as increased ammunition stowage for the 12.7mm machine guns, and internal automotive improvements.

In 1955, it was decided to develop a new heavy assault gun on the T-10 chassis. Designated Obiekt 268, the conversion consisted of a simple box structure mounting an improved 152mm gun-howitzer with a bore-evacuator. The prototype of the Obiekt 268 went through trials in 1956. However, there was some doubt about the need for such a vehicle in view of the large numbers of ISU-152s already in service, and the design was not accepted for production.

In the late 1950s, the Kotin Design Bureau at the Kirov plant in Leningrad were assigned their final heavy artillery project, based on Stalin tank components. The programme was a direct response to the US Army's 280mm 'atomic cannon'. Two seperate versions were built on the izdeliye 271 chassis. The Kondensator 2P was armed with the Grabin SM-54 406mm gun and had a range of 28 km. The Oka was armed with a Shayvrin 420mm breech-loaded mortar that could fire nuclear projectiles 45 km. Both vehicles weighed about 55 tons, and had a low rate of fire,

one round every five minutes. The maximum range of both these weapons was estimated by US intelligence to be over 25 km. The Oka was modernised and a new variant appeared in the 1960 October Revolution parade in Moscow. Their service was very short-lived. They served in the special artillery regiments of the High Command Reserve (RVGK), but they were difficult to transport and their performance on the test ranges was poor. They were retired in the early 1960s as effective tactical ballistic missiles such as the R-11 (Scud) and Luna (FROG-3) became available.

Missile vehicles

In 1954, the Korolev OKB-1 design bureau in Kaliningrad developed the first Soviet tactical ballistic missile, the R-11. The R-11 was intended for the delivery of tactical nuclear warheads. The Kirov bureau in Leningrad was assigned the task of developing a suitable chassis for transporting and launching the missile. This system was called the 8K11, and basically consisted of an IS heavy tank chassis with a modified superstructure containing the launch equipment, missile erector, and associated equipment called the ZU 218. These were referred to as SS-1b Scud A by Western intelligence. The 8K11 were organised into operational-tactical missile brigades which consisted of three launch battalions, each with three 8K11 vehicles. These brigades were assigned at army level and about 100 launcher vehicles were built. In the late 1950s, the Makeyev design bureau in Miass developed an improved version of the R-11 missile, called the R-17 Zemlya (Earth). This missile was longer than the R-11 and required a modified launcher. The Kotin design bureau modernised the 8K11 system as the 8K11/8K14. This basically meant that the launcher vehicle could fire either missile. The latter type is called SS-1c Scud B in the West. The 8K11/8K14 was deployed with Soviet units in 1961.

The ZU 218 launcher vehicle based on the IS heavy tank chassis was not entirely suitable, causing a significant problem to the systems on board due to vibration. In addition, production of the IS chassis had already ended. As a result, a new launcher, the 9P117, was developed on the basis

The 8K11/14 was an improved version of the ZU 218 tactical ballistic missile launcher which could also fire the longer Makeyev R-17 Zemlya missile (SS-1c Scud B). It was replaced in 1965 by the 9P117 launch vehicle, based on the MAZ-543 heavy wheeled transporter.

of the MAZ-543 heavy wheeled transporter. This first appeared in 1965 and became the standard type of Scud launcher.

The IS heavy tank chassis was also used as the launcher for unguided tactical ballistic rockets in the early 1950s, called FROG-1 (Free Rocket Over Ground-1) in the West. The first of these rockets, possibly designated Mars, was developed by the Ganichev design bureau and appeared in 1957. The launcher vehicle for this system resembled the 8K11, but had the rocket completely enclosed in a large tubular structure. This particular rocket system was not very successful, and appears to have vanished from the scene by the end of the 1950s. In its place, the Kotin design bureau developed a more mobile launcher, based on the PT-76 light tank.

Recovery vehicles

The weight of IS heavy tanks and ISU assault guns led to the need for dedicated recovery vehicles. At first, turretless KV heavy tanks were used in this role. However, by the end of the war, spare parts for these vehicles became an increasing difficulty, and there were not enough KV hulls for the rapidly expanding heavy tank and assault gun force. As an interim solution, in 1945 a number of uncompleted IS-2 tanks were converted into improvised recovery vehicles designated the IS-2T (T–*tyagach*, tractor). This was basically a turretless IS-2m. In the 1950s, some vehicles had the turret ring plated over, and a cupola from the IS-2 tank added. In the 1960s, after the IS-2M was withdrawn from active service, many of the chassis were retained as recovery vehicles. The turret ring was plated over, and the tank commander's cupola was added on the left side.

The first serious effort at developing a heavy armoured recovery vehicle took place in the 1950s. With the withdrawal of the ISU-122 from service as part of a programme to standardise on the ISU-152, many ISU-122 hulls became redundant. The first series of recovery vehicles, called ISU-T, simply had the gun removed, and the opening plated over. In 1959, a more serious programme was undertaken, patterned after the German Bergepanzer, and its Soviet counterpart, the BTS-2 on the T-54A chassis. These recovery vehicles were designated as the BTT-1 (*bronirovanniy tyazheliy tyagach*, armoured heavy tractor). As in the case of the ISU-T, the gun was removed and the opening plated over. A large tool platform was added at the rear of the chassis, and a heavy winch was installed in the fighting compartment. At the rear was a large spade to fix the vehicle in position when using the winch. In 1960, a modernisation programme was begun, called BTT-1T which added an additional generator to the vehicle to assist in welding and other field repairs. There was a certain amount of variation on BTT-1s in service. In some units, the BTT-1 was locally modernised by the addition of an A-frame crane.

The only other country to receive any extensive number of ISU-152s was Egypt, which purchased at least one regiment in the early 1960s. The Israeli Army encountered a small number of these in the 1967 and 1973 wars, as well as the related BTT-1 recovery vehicles. In later years, they were dug in as semi-static defensive positions along the Suez Canal.

The most widely distributed Stalin tank variant was the 8K11 and 8K11/8K14 missile launcher. Poland, Czechoslovakia, East Germany, Romania, Hungary and Bulgaria were all sold these systems in 1960-1 as part of a general Warsaw Pact modernization programme. Poland, Czechoslovakia and East Germany replaced them in the late 1960s for the more reliable 9P117 Uragan launcher, based on the MAZ-543 wheeled transporter. So far as is known, all exports of the R-17 missile system outside of the Warsaw Pact included the 9P117 launcher. There have been some reports, however, that Iraq received at least one 8K11/14 launcher for training purposes.

VARIANTS IN FOREIGN SERVICE

Although the Stalin tanks were not widely exported, a significant number of their variants were exported. As in the case of the IS-2 tanks, the largest user of Stalin derivatives during the Second World War was the Polish People's Army (LWP). The LWP formed a single ISU-122 unit, the 25th self-propelled Artillery Regiment. This unit was committed as part of the 1st Polish Armoured Corps to the Nysa River battles starting in March 1945. Another heavy regiment was planned, but insufficient ISU-152s were available. As a result, the 13th Self-propelled Artillery Regiment was formed as a composite regiment with two batteries of SU-85 medium assault guns and two batteries of ISU-152s. This unit took part in the Berlin campaign in May 1945. Both the ISU-122 and ISU-152 remained in Polish service after the war and a small number were converted into recovery vehicles in the late 1960s.

THE PLATES

Plate A: *IS-2 Model 1944, 104th Tank Regiment, 7th Guards Novgorodskiy Tank Brigade, Berlin, May 1945*
Soviet tanks during the Second World War were uniformly painted in very dark green. In 1944-45, tactical insignia began to be applied more widely, mainly to assist in traffic control during offensive operations. This IS-2 shows the elaborate markings sometimes seen towards the end of the war. The white turret bands and white roof cross were part of an April 1945 agreement between the Red Army and Anglo-American military leaders to prevent Allied fighter bombers from attacking Soviet armoured columns as the two forces met in Germany. On 29 April 1945, the Soviets found a German tank marked with these insignia, so it was decided to change the insignia to a large white triangle on the roof and a small white triangle on the turret sides. However, this second change did not take place in significant numbers until later in May during the Prague operation. During the

Berlin operation, the white turret cross was the predominant air identification marking.

The 7th Guards Tank Brigade's insignia was a white polar bear on a red star. The badge was a result of the brigade's earlier service. At the time of the German invasion this unit was the 46th Tank Division of the 21st Mechanised Corps operating in the Baltic area. After the defeats of 1941, it was reorganised as the 46th Tank Brigade and fought in the Leningrad area. It was renamed as the 7th Guards in 1944 in recognition of its combat performance and took part in the offensive against Finland in the summer of that year. In November 1944 the brigade fought against German troops around Petsamo in the Arctic circle. It was this campaign that the polar bear insignia commemorated. After returning from the far North, the brigade turned in its T-34 tanks and was re-equipped with IS-2 Stalin tanks. It was as one of the new heavy tank brigades that it fought in the last offensives against Germany, and took part in the fighting in the centre of Berlin.

The brigade had three regiments, the 104th, 105th and 106th. So the first digit of the tactical number on the turret identified the regiment, in this case, the 104th Tank Regiment. This particular tank had a name on the turret rear, *Boyevaya Podruga*, 'Friend in Battle'.

Plate B1: *IS-2 Model 1944, Polish 4th Heavy Tank Regiment, Berlin area, 1945*
The Polish units fighting alongside the Red Army followed similar markings practices. The white turret band and roof cross are typical of IS-2 heavy tanks during the Berlin operation. The unit insignia is a white Piast eagle, on a red rhomboid. The eagle insignia was the Polish communist national emblem, a variation on the traditional Polish national eagle insignia, minus its 'royal' crown. The red rhomboid is at once a communist insignia and a reminder of the Polish national colours (red and white). In addition it was a symbol familiar to any Red Army tanker, as the rhomboid was the standard Russian map symbol designating an armoured unit. The tactical numbering system used on the turret side followed Soviet practices.

Plate B2: *IS-2 Model 1944, 78th Guards Heavy Tank Regiment, Jihlava, Czechoslovakia, 1945*
This is a fairly typical style of markings for independent heavy tank regiments. The number is usually only two digits, since the regiment is so small. In this case, all 21 tanks of the regiment may have been numbered sequentially. The regimental insignia is a yellow Cyrillic 'D' in a rhomboid. The significance of the 'D' in the insignia is not known.

C1: *ISU-122S, 2nd Belorussian Front, Gdansk, February 1945*
This ISU-122S served with an unidentified heavy assault gun regiment during the capture of Gdansk (Danzig). The markings consist of a standard two digit tactical number, probably indicating the 3rd vehicle of the 2nd battery, and an honorific *Imeni Mikoyan* which means 'Named after Mikoyan'. The honorific probably refers to Anastas Mikoyan, one of Stalin's closest advisors. These days, it is the other brother who is better known, Artem Mikoyan, who designed the MiG fighters.

C2: *ISU-152, Guards Heavy Assault Gun Brigade, April 1945*
This ISU-152 from an unidentified brigade shows more elaborate markings than usual. The side slogan reads *Osvobozhdennaya Kirovskaya*, or 'Liberated Kirovskiy', while the tactical number is unusual in that it is edged in red. The high number probably indicates a brigade formation rather than a regiment. Usually, the first number in a two-digit code indicated battery: 1, 2 or 3 for the batteries of the 1st battalion, 4,5 or 6 for the batteries of the 2nd battalion, etc. On the upper front of the superstructure is this tactical unit insignia in white. Its precise origins are not known, but it is similar to several map emblems. Red Army tactical insignia were devised locally and were intentionally kept simple to reduce their value to German intelligence.

D: *IS-2 Model 1944, 95th Guards Independent Heavy Tank Regiment, Berlin, 1945*
The IS-2 adopted a hull configuration which remained standard until the 1960s. The previous

KV heavy tank series had two crewmen in the front of the hull, a driver and machine gunner/radio operator. The second crewman was dropped to save space and permit a better armoured bow. The radio was moved to the commander's station in the turret and the hull machine gun was made fixed and operated by the driver. Although a fixed machine gun might not seem very accurate, tankers who have used it insist that they could easily hit a target the size of a fuel drum with a single burst. The turret contained the remainder of the crew: the commander in the left rear of the turret, the gunner in front of him and the loader on the right side. The ammunition was a two-piece type, with the projectiles stowed vertically in racks in the rear turret bustle. The propellant cases were stowed in metal boxes on the floor of the fighting compartment. The D-25T 122mm gun had a co-axial 7.62mm DTM machine gun on the right side, accessible to the gunner for reloading. There was aan additional ball-mounted DTM in a projection on the left rear of the turret. The engine was located immediately behind the fighting compartment, followed by the cooling system and transmission. The running gear on the IS-2 was much the same as the KV series with torsion bar suspension and a rear-mounted drive sprocket.

E: *T-10M, Guards Heavy Tank self-propelled Regiment, Operation Danube, Prague, Czechoslovakia, 1968*

This T-10M is finished in markings typical of Operation Danube, the invasion of Czechoslovakia in 1968. Soviet tank markings were usually very simple in the 1960s, usually limited to a set of white tactical numbers on the hull side. During operations, more elaborate tactical insignia reminiscent of wartime insignia was adopted to help manage road and rail movements. In this case, the insignia is painted in white on a black rectangle. The geometric shape was often assigned systematically within a division or army, and in this case is a large diamond. The numbering varies in meaning. In this case the 5-10/37 probably has the following meaning: 5 is the regiment's convoy number, -10 is convoy serial, and 37 is the tactical number for a tank of the 3rd company, 3rd platoon (1st platoon is 1-3, second is 4-6, third is 7-9). The Operation Danube invasion markings are similar to those used in Berlin in 1945 and were adopted to distinguish invading tanks from Czechoslovak tanks. They consisted of white bands on the turret roof which resembled a cross when viewed from above. The bands extended on to the hull, going down the hull sides, bow and rear.

F1: *IS-3M, Egyptian 4th Armoured Division, Cairo, 1967*

This court division in Cairo was frequently used for parades, and was painted in elaborate markings for show. In this case, the division's heavy tank regiment was painted with a royal vulture insignia, reminiscent of the insignia found in the ancient sites of the pharaohs. These insignia were not used in combat. IS-3Ms encountered in the 1967 war in the Sinai were generally devoid of markings and painted simply in overall light sand colour.

F2: *ISU-152, Genifa Hills defence line, Suez Canal Zone, 1973*

By the time of the Yom Kippur War, many of the IS-3M and ISU-152s were camouflage painted. The scheme generally consisted of the normal light sand colour, oversprayed with a pattern of dark green, and a slightly pinkish red-brown colour. This particular vehicle was part of a static defence line in the Genifa Hills south of Ismailya overlooking the Suez Canal.

G: *IS-3, Coastal Defence Unit, Kurile Islands, 1992*

Many IS-3 and T-10 tanks remain in service in the Russian Far East in static defensive positions. Some of these tanks are still in running condition, but many are completely dug in. This particular example was driven into an entrenchment overlooking the beaches facing Japan to act as a coastal defence pill-box. The tank was finished in a medium green colour, lighter than usual due to the fading effects of the sun, with a large rolling pattern of medium brown sprayed over it. There were no unit markings since they would be inappropriate for this role.

Notes sur les planches en couleurs

A On voit sur cet IS-2 les marques compliquées utilisées vers la fin de la guerre. Les rayures blanches sur la tourelle et la croix blanche sur le toit sont là pour empêcher les bombardiers alliés d'attaquer les chars soviétiques. En 1945 ces insignes furent changées en un triangle blanc sur le toit et un triangle plus petit sur les côtés de la tourelle. L'insigne de la 7ème brigade de gardes blindés était un ours polaire, en souvenir du service de cette Brigade au cercle arctique en 1944.

B1 Cet IS-2 appartenait à une unité polonaise mais présente des marques similaires à celles des chars de l'Armée Rouge. L'insigne de cette unité est un aigle Piast blanc sur un rhomboïde rouge. Le numéro tactique sur le côté de la tourelle est conforme aux habitudes soviétiques. **B2** Un char du 78ème régiment des gardes blindés lourds avec des marques de style typiques des régiments blindés lourds indépendants. L'insigne régimentale est un 'D' cyrillique jaune dans un rhomboïde.

C1 Cet ISU-122S servit avec un régiment de canonniers d'assaut lourds durant la capture de Gdansk. Ses marques sont composées d'un numéro tactique de deux chffres et d'un *Imeni Mikoyan* honorifique qui signifie 'Porte le nom de Mikoyan'. **C2** Un ISU-152 avec des marques compliquées. Le numéro tactique est entouré de rouge, ce qui n'est pas habituel. A l'avant de la superstructure, en haut, on trouve l'insigne tactique de l'unité en blanc.

D L'IS-2 adoptait une configuration de coque qui resta standard jusqu'aux années 60. Un membre d'équipage à l'avant, une radio dans la tourelle et une mitrailleuse fixe sous le contrôle du pilote. La tourelle contenait le reste de l'équipage. La réserve de munitions était en deux parties et les projectiles étaient stockés sur des rangées dans la courbe arrière de la tourelle. Le moteur était situé juste derrière le compartiment de combat.

E Ce T-10M est fini avec des marques typiques de l'invasion de la Tchécoslovaquie en 1968. L'insigne, un gros diamant, est peint en blanc sur un rectangle noir. Les marques d'invasion du char sont composées de rayures blanches sur le toit de la tourelle qui ressemblent à une croix lorsqu'on les voit du dessus.

F1 La 4ème division blindée au Caire était souvent utilisée pour les parades et ses chars portaient des marques compliquées. Le régiment blindé lourd de la division portait comme insigne un vautour royal (pas utilisé pour le combat). Les IS-3M durant la guerre de 1967 au Sinai portaient rarement des marques. Ils étaient peints en couleur sable clair de manière uniforme. **F2** A l'époque de la guerre du Yom Kippur, la majorité des IS-3M et des ISU-152 étaient peints en motifs camouflage. . Il s'agissait de la couleur sable clair normal avec une surcouche de motifs verts et marron rougeâtre un peu rosé.

G Ce char a été conduit dans un retranchement pour jouer le rôle de blockhaus de défense côtière dans les îles Kurile (1992). Fini en vert moyen (rendu plus clair par le soleil) avec un motif marron par dessus. Ne comporte pas de marques d'unité.

Farbtafeln

A Auf diesem IS-2 sieht man die kunstvolle Kennzeichnung, die gegen Ende des Krieges auftauchte. Die weißen Streifen auf dem Panzerturm und Kreuz auf dem Dach sollten verhindern, daß die Jagdbomber der Alliierten die sowjetischen Panzer angriffen. 1945 wurde das Zeichen durch ein weißes Dreieck auf dem Dach und ein kleineres Dreieck an den Seiten des Panzerturms ersetzt. Das Zeichen der 7. Panzerbrigade war ein Eisbär, was daran erinnerte, daß die Brigaden 1944 am nördlichen Polarkreis Dienst getan hatten.

B1 Dieser IS-2 gehörte einer polnischen Einheit an, weist jedoch eine Kennzeichnung auf, die der auf den Panzern der Roten Armee ähnlich ist. Das Kennzeichen der Einheit ist ein weißer Adler auf einem roten Parallelogramm. Die taktische Nummer auf der Seite des Panzerturms folgt dem sowjetischen Muster. **B2** Ein Panzer des 78. schweren Panzerregiments mit den typischen Kennzeichnen für unabhängige, schwere Panzerregimenter. Das Regimentsabzeichen ist ein gelbes, kyrillisches "D" in einem Parallelogramm.

C1 Dieser ISU-122S gehörte zu einem schweren Strumgeschütz-Regiment bei der Einnahme von Gdansk. Seine Kennzeichnung besteht aus der üblichen, zweistelligen taktischen Nummer und dem Ehrentitel *Imeni Mikoyan*, was "nach Mikoyan benannt" bedeutet. **C2** Ein ISU-152 mit kunstvoller Kennzeichnung. Ungewöhnlicherweise ist die taktische Nummer in rot eingefaßt. Auf der oberen Vorderseite des Aufbaus steht das Zeichen der Kampfeinheit in weiß.

D Der IS-2 erhielt einen Rumpfbau, der bis in die 60er Jahre zur Norm wurde. Ein Besatzungsmitglied sitzt vorne, im Panzerturm befindet sich ein Funkgerät und ein feststehendes Maschinengewehr, das vom Fahrer bedient wird. Der Rest der Besatzung ist im Panzerturm. Die Munition war zweiteilig, und die Geschosse wurden in Ständern im hinteren Teil des Panzerturms aufbewahrt. Der Motor befindet sich unmittelbar hinter dem Gefechtsstand.

E Dieser T-10M weist die Kennzeichen auf, die für den Einmarsch in der Tschechoslowakei 1968 typisch waren. Das Zeichen, ein großer Rhombus, ist in weiß auf ein schwarzes Rechteck gemalt. Die Invasionszeichen des Panzers bestehen aus weißen Streifen auf dem Dach des Panzerturms, die von oben gesehen einem Kreuz gleichen.

F1 Die 4. Panzerdivision in Kairo wurde häufig bei Paraden eingesetzt, und die Panzer wurden mit kunstvollen Kennzeichen bemalt. Das schwere Panzerregiment der Division war mit einem königlichen Geier-Emblem bemalt (nicht im Gefecht). IS-3Ms im Krieg 1967 auf der Halbinsel Sinai wiesen selten Kennzeichen auf und waren einfarbig hellsandfarben. **F2** Beim Jom-Kippur-Krieg waren viele der IS-3M und der ISU-152 in Tarnfarben gespritzt, das heißt, die Grundfarbe war hellbeige und mit einem dunkelgrünen und leicht rosa-rotbraunen Muster übersprüht.

G Dieser Panzer wurde in eine Verschanzung gefahren, wo er auf den Kurilen (1992) als Bunker der Küstenverteidigung diente. Er ist mittelgrün (inzwischen in der Sonne verblichen) und hat darüber ein braunes Muster. Er weist keinerlei Kennzeichen der Einheit auf.